PRESUMED GUILTY

Talked to Death: The Life & Murder of Alan Berg

A Killing in the Family

Notre Dame's Greatest Coaches

Sweet Evil

Charmed to Death

*Legacy of Deception: An Investigation
of Mark Fuhrman and Racism in the L.A.P.D.*

*Power to Burn: Michael Ovitz
and the New Business of Show Business*

The Rise and Rise of David Geffen

PRESUMED GUILTY

An Investigation into the JonBenet Ramsey Case, the Media, and the Culture of Pornography

Stephen Singular

New Millennium Press

BEVERLY HILLS

ISBN: 1-893224-00-7

Printed in the United States of America

New Millennium Press
a division of New Millennium Entertainment
350 S. Beverly Drive
Suite 315
Beverly Hills, California 90212

10 9 8 7 6 5 4 3 2 1

To Donald and Patty Freed,
Lee Hill and Alan Katz

This book is intended to raise more questions than it answers—questions that have thus far been publicly ignored. Most of what follows is fact, but some is conjecture, based on what is currently known. The future will reveal how much of it is true.

Contents

Acknowledgments   *xi*

Prologue   I

part one   Going to Boulder   13

part two   Lost in Cyberspace   43

part three   The Summertime Blues   145

part four   Waiting   221

Epilogue   239

Acknowledgments

Books are collaborative processes. Many valuable discussions formed this book, although most of them don't appear in these pages. I was repeatedly assisted by conversations with Pam Griffin and her daughter, Kristine; by talks with Evan Ravitz, Duncan Campbell, and Bob McFarland; and by provocative question-and-answer sessions with Lawrence Schiller and Bob Richards. The book's editor, Shelly Kale, helped bring a difficult subject into better focus, while my wife, Joyce, dropped some useful intuitions along the way.

The Boulder authorities were at least willing to listen and to consider that there were things about the Ramsey case that they had not yet uncovered. They deserve credit for that. So do Deborah Raffin and Michael Viner, the publishers of New Millennium Press, for being open to alternative explorations of a great mystery.

PRESUMED GUILTY

Prologue

The evening of January 9, 1997, was bitter cold in Boulder, Colorado, with the temperature already below zero and headed down. The frozen earth snapped when you stepped on it, the air gnawed at your cheeks, and breathing hurt your teeth. Normally such weather would have kept people inside, but not tonight. Three hundred journalists and support personnel had arrived in town from both coasts, England, Australia, and the Far East. ABC television, for example, had sent twenty people, including on-air journalists, network executives from New York, and private investigators who had just been put on the payroll. Hotels and restaurants were full, sidewalks were crowded, and the community had the buzz that comes when the collective media focuses its attention on a single place and for a single reason. Everyone was asking everyone else the same question: Who killed six-year-old JonBenet Ramsey, the little beauty queen found sexually assaulted and strangled to death with a garotte in the basement of her parents' home on the day after Christmas?

The Ramsey residence was just a few blocks away from the Boulder Public Library, where one hundred reporters were now gathering for the first nationally televised press conference on the case. The event was scheduled for 7:00 P.M. and by 6:45, scores of people were milling in the brutally cold lobby, trading business cards, renewing old acquaintances—many had recently covered the O.J. Simpson trial in Los

I

Angeles—and laughing at jokes about rich families and murdered children.

If war protests and rock concerts defined the American sixties, if sex parties characterized the seventies, and if monied affairs distinguished the eighties, then what was unfolding in Boulder tonight illustrated the very symbol of our national preoccupation with crime in the nineties. Since the fall of the Soviet Union, no international news stories had rivaled the coverage of our domestic crimes—the Menendez brothers case, the Susan Smith case, the O.J. Simpson case, the Oklahoma City bombing case, and now, the JonBenet Ramsey case. We had turned our attention inward with a vengeance and an overkill that had reached comic proportions. In the library's lobby this evening, photographers were snapping pictures of journalists who were interviewing other reporters who were talking to TV personnel who were taping their words that would be presented later to their audiences as news.

Something much larger than a series of murders was happening across America, something strange and subtle and hard to define, something potentially dangerous. In decades past, during high-profile criminal cases, the media and the public had mostly acted as observers of the legal system. They had stood back and respected the rules and often-tedious, time-consuming rituals of that system. They had seen themselves as one part—and not the most important part—of a significant social process. They had exercised self-control. By the mid-nineties, mostly as a result of the Simpson case, this had begun to change in ways that were corrosive and frightening, yet the change had been normalized to such a degree that it had hardly been noticed.

On this night it would finally become too obvious to ignore.

* * *

The Boulder police chief, Tom Koby, had handpicked five local reporters to ask him questions in a warm wing of the library while the rest of the journalists remained in the lobby. Shortly after 7:00, when Koby's face appeared on the lobby's TV monitors, the reporters stopped milling and fell silent. They gazed up at the chief, a few of them snickering and ridiculing his appearance. Koby had a salt-and-pepper beard, impatient eyes, and a soft, southern voice. Facing the camera, he looked nervous and quietly enraged, as if he despised what he was doing this evening—public relations—and despised the media and everyone who worked for it.

Many people in the lobby were in a bad mood, but not because they were freezing. JonBenet Ramsey had been dead for fourteen days and the Boulder authorities had not yet arrested her wealthy parents as the alleged killers. Why the delay? The body had been discarded in the Ramseys' basement, hadn't it? The ransom note found in their home had clearly been phony, right? Didn't that obviously make John and Patsy Ramsey guilty of murder?

Peter Boyles, a Denver radio talk show host who was mingling in the lobby, was certain that it did. In upcoming weeks, he would step forward as the loudest and most shrill voice demanding the Ramseys' heads. He knew they belonged in prison, and would not stop at demonizing them. He would also castigate the town of Boulder, its citizens, its officials, and any reporter or caller to his show who dared to disagree with him. He didn't need to see the evidence before reaching his conclusions, and within a few months he would be promoting his convictions not just on local radio but on the nation's television airwaves as well, becoming a star commentator and pushing his anger everywhere.

Long before JonBenet was killed, Boyles and many other members of the media had expressed their rage at the acquittal of O.J. Simpson, another wealthy man accused of murder, in October 1995 in Los Angeles. The overwhelmingly white mainstream press and public, unshakably convinced of Simpson's guilt, had been shocked by this outcome. Instead of questioning their own assumptions and opinions about the case, instead of reexamining the evidence, they had hardened their view that the mostly African-American jurors had been dead wrong or dead stupid. Anybody with an I.Q. above room temperature, Boyles liked to say on the air, knew exactly what had occurred in L.A.: Simpson had gotten away with a double murder. That logic had immediately carried over to Boulder: Because O.J. had been guilty, the Ramseys were guilty, too.

This implied, of course, that Boyles was much more intelligent than the people who had actually listened to all the evidence—the jurors. It also implied that he was much smarter than two members of Simpson's winning legal team: Barry Scheck, one of the nation's leading attorneys who specialize in DNA, and Dr. Henry Lee, director of the Connecticut State Forensic Science Laboratory, who was generally regarded as the most astute observer of crime evidence in the world. Dr. Lee's famous courtroom pronouncement after looking at the evidence in the Simpson case summed it up quickly and well: "Something wrong."

Simpson's acquittal had altered America. It would be impossible to overestimate the effect the case had on journalism, talk radio, race relations, book publishing, public commentary about the legal system, the legal system itself, and the citizenry. Our society had never been presented with a better opportunity to examine itself and its media, and there had never been more resistance to engaging in such an endeavor. Talk radio and talk TV participants set the tone for what followed the verdict: Close your ears and blame the jurors for not being as bright as you are. The legacy of that resistance and that anger was the scorn that would soon be directed at Police Chief Tom Koby.

In his opening remarks, the chief noted that there was an "inherent conflict" between the police and the media in these circumstances: The cops wanted to find the girl's murderer and the press just wanted a quick solution to the case. Some of the people in the lobby pointed their fingers up at the monitors and began to laugh. Koby's next statement, that the media's intense focus on the tragedy revealed a "sick curiosity," was greeted with whistling and catcalls. When the chief said that his department solved 85 percent of its homicides, as opposed to a nationwide success rate of 65 percent, the crowd began to boo and moan.

"Why the hell haven't you solved this one?" somebody yelled.

"Because he's afraid of big, bad John Ramsey and his money, that's why," someone answered, to applause and laughter.

Koby threw out some more statistics, but the journalists' attention was already starting to drift.

"JonBenet was killed in a satanic ritual," one said. "It was planned by her parents for Christmas night."

"The mother's into kinky sex," said another. "You can tell just by looking at her."

"The father's a pedophile," somebody added. "She was starting to talk about what he was doing to her, so he strangled her to keep her quiet."

"John Ramsey flies a private plane," said one more. "I bet he takes drugs back and forth across the Mexican border and he pissed off some of his connections down there and ..."

A picture of the dead girl, Koby was saying, had been hung on a wall at the police station to remind his detectives why they were working so hard on this case. He then suggested that the local populace, which according to many reports had been deeply upset by this murder, might want to get some therapy in order to cope with their stress.

"You need therapy, asshole!" a journalist in the lobby shouted.

"And a fuckin' brain!"

"Why don't you arrest the parents, Koby?"

The chief, almost as if he could hear these comments, stared into the camera and said, "We are not going to have this case tried in the media."

"Too late for that!" a reporter in the lobby responded, and others giggled.

"Just back off a little bit," Koby continued, "and let us do our jobs."

"If we back off," a woman called out, "you'll stop doing your job."

She was quickly surrounded by cheers.

I had come to the press conference from Denver that evening as an observer and a freelance writer. Now I stood in a corner of the lobby and listened to the running commentary. The feeling in the room was unlike anything I had ever encountered and I couldn't immediately identify it, because it didn't have any of the usual trappings. Nobody was holding a gun or ax handle. Nobody was wearing a uniform or being stirred by the rhetoric of a gifted speaker. Nobody looked downtrodden or oppressed. These people were well educated, well paid, and highly successful, even celebrities in their chosen fields. They were middle-class, mainstream Americans, but at the moment they were trashing one of the most basic principles of our legal system—the presumption of innocence—and acting like a mob bent on imposing its rule on others.

I was taken aback. Thirteen years earlier, I'd begun working on a book about Alan Berg, a Denver talk show host who had been assassinated by neo-Nazis. The word most frequently attached to Berg's old radio persona had been "obnoxious." He was usually prickly with callers and at times downright nasty, hanging up on many people. Despite his antics, his audience mostly perceived him as a humorous, colorful novelty, an oddball whom no one took very seriously. Talk radio was still young and innocent, just a bunch of folks having a telephone conversation that was being broadcast to others. Berg was one of its more provocative talents, "the man you love to hate," but you were supposed to hate him only in the context of entertainment.

Twelve bullets pumped into his face and body at point-blank range on the evening of June 18, 1984, ended all that. Berg's assassination in his driveway signaled the moment when talk radio grew up: It was now perceived as potent enough, and threatening enough, to compel an organized cadre of extremists to kill one of its practitioners. By the mid-nineties, the talk show had become the most popular form of AM radio and was even more successful on television. Its stars were instantly recognizable by their first names only—Oprah, Howard, Sally, Jessy, Rush, Larry, and Jerry—and its effects on bending and shaping public consciousness were immeasurable.

While researching Berg's death, I had become quite familiar with absolutism and intolerance. I had documented what happened when people came together in order to demonize others and blame them out of spite and unexamined rage. I had chronicled what occurred once the language of violence became acceptable—that it was all right to hate "niggers" and Jews and homosexuals and anyone else whom you were convinced was evil or dangerous. Once that belief was in place, somebody had begun shooting the enemy.

Since 1990, I had written four other books about murder cases, but as I studied the faces in the lobby of the Boulder Public Library that evening, I realized that homicides were no longer the story. *We* were—the media, the talk shows, the American public, and our response to the violence around us. The mindset that had killed Alan Berg had somehow seeped out from a tiny fringe group of neo-Nazis and infected the mainstream itself, which was now clamoring for an arrest out of its own anger and impatience. How had this happened? How could we so easily disregard the constitutional rights and privileges that we had lived by for the past 220 years? Why were we so willing to blame people before we knew the facts? When had our minds become sealed, and what had been done to us to make us act this way?

Strangely enough, I couldn't fit any of these questions into a political or economic context. This phenomenon was occurring during one of the most peaceful and prosperous times in American history, but neither peace nor affluence seemed to make any difference. The need to blame and demonize cut across all class, race, sex, and educational lines. It was a general condition of our decade, reinforced every day and every night—on talk radio in particular—and reflecting a new psychological and emotional reality.

Were we becoming, without even being aware of it, more like the machines we had created to observe us, the TV cameras now largely responsible for mirroring our world back to us? Those machines could only show surfaces and those surfaces were now shaping us in ways we hadn't even begun to comprehend. Cameras functioned without empathy or compassion or discernment or flexibilty, without critical thinking or emotional intelligence or intuition, without any of the things that make us human beings.

Walking out of the library on that frigid evening, I assumed that Chief Koby and his people would soon solve the Ramsey case. I was more intrigued with other questions. How far down this road to blame had we gone and where was it leading us? What was the human cost of this mindset and what did it imply for our nation's future as a democracy?

As it turned out, I was wrong about the JonBenet murder investigation. Eighteen months after Chief Koby's first press conference, the homicide had not been solved and very little new information had emerged. We were still looking at surfaces. Between January 1997 and July 1998, I became involved in that investigation, traveling to Boulder many times and meeting some of the key individuals in the case. What I learned was often alarming but always educational. I couldn't find a demon over there, just a lot of human beings with good intentions and frailties, trying to make sense of an increasingly disturbing world.

During that year and a half, another development, somewhat related to the Ramsey case, erupted. Bill Clinton, the president of the United States, began receiving the same treatment as O.J. Simpson, Richard Jewell (the falsely accused suspect in the 1996 bombing at the Olympic games in Atlanta), and John and Patsy Ramsey. After allegations of a sexual affair with White House intern Monica Lewinsky were reported in January 1998, countless people on talk radio and talk TV charged forward and presumed the president guilty—not simply of infidelity or terrible judgment, which was fair enough, but of all manner of things that were criminally wrong and detrimental to the country. What these critics themselves were doing to America was rarely discussed.

The press liked to refer to Mr. Clinton as "the most powerful man on earth," but what power did he have to prevent commentators like talk show host Rush Limbaugh, and a hundred other imitators, from viciously attacking him and the First Lady day after day on the nation's airwaves—stating to a huge audience that the Clintons were guilty of sins and crimes alike, although nothing had been proven against them using due process in a court of law? What power did the president have to exercise his Fifth Amendment right to protection from self-incrimination, when media pundits constantly analyzed his voice, his image, and his mannerisms before concluding that he had been involved in immoral or illegal activities?

What power did he have to exert his Sixth Amendment right to a speedy resolution of his legal difficulties, when special prosecutor Kenneth Starr, financed by nearly $50 million in public monies, could investigate him at the most personal level for more than four years in order to find *something* to accuse him of? The grand inquisitor had now arrived, with a blue nose and a sexual microscope. What power did the president have to stop Starr from using illicitly obtained telephone conversations against him? And what power did he have to employ his Seventh Amendment right to an impartial jury when the entire population of the United States had repeatedly heard him charged with wrongdoing—by those who did not know what he actually had or had not done?

Millions upon millions of talk show listeners were now

publicly encouraged to express their hatred of the president, as they had been encouraged to do earlier with O.J. Simpson and the Ramseys. An uncivil war had started and it would soon turn bitterly political.

The disorder lurking right beneath the skin of our society was spreading apace, and some people were beginning to take notice. After watching the media's endless coverage of the Clinton-Lewinsky brouhaha, which had uncovered nothing new for months and months, consumer advocate Ralph Nader called the press clinically insane. After hearing that three hundred journalists had shown up to report on Linda Tripp's grand jury testimony in the Starr investigation, Oakland's mayor and former presidential hopeful Jerry Brown described the media's focus on the story as "nothing more than their attempt to sell soft-core pornography." Social critic and author Michael Lerner, the editor of *Tikkun* magazine, went even further, asserting that the media's total inability to distinguish what was significant from what was not had destroyed American public life, emptying it of seriousness and value.

On January 21, 1998, the same day the Clinton-Lewinsky story broke and began holding the media hostage for the forseeable future, forty-four officers from five law-enforcement agencies were charged with taking money to protect cocaine trafficking operations in Cleveland and northern Ohio. These arrests were not isolated; they were the latest in a string of investigations that from 1994 to 1997 resulted in the conviction of 508 officers in forty-seven cities. Was there another development in the country that could tell us more about the violence, the temptations, the corruption, and the underlying contradictions of our culture? No, but this story simply could not compete with the titilating notion of a president having sex with a younger woman, so it was buried under the rubble of erotic journalism. The Tabloid Decade had found its ultimate tale.

Our culture—like Ken Starr himself—had embraced a double standard: We were more nervous about sex but more accepting of pornography. The latter tendency filtered out in many different directions. It pervaded the political climate. It influenced chic advertising. It ran rampant on the Internet and clung to the atmosphere surrounding child beauty pageants. It contributed to the widespread sexualization of young girls and affected the media coverage of the Ramsey case, just as it had once touched JonBenet's life itself. The bigger question was: Had it also helped to kill her?

part one

Going to Boulder

1

A great sea once covered the Front Range of Colorado, but over hundreds of millennia, the water receded, the earth convulsed, and huge slabs of brownish rock shot up from the ground. In 1858, miners struck gold in these mountains, known as the Flatirons, and white settlers made camp nearby in a village called Boulder City. Its sixty original shareholders established the first school in Colorado and righteously enforced frontier justice. Murderers were hanged in public, while horse thieves were given twenty-one bare-back lashes and had one side of their heads shaved so that everyone could recognize the criminals walking among them. Boulder, as the town came to be called, expanded and grew right under the shadows of the Flatirons, which rose up behind the community, sheer and vast and the color of dried blood, like tablets of stone driven straight into the land.

Whenever I came into Boulder from the east on Highway 36 and took in this vista, my heart caught and I felt humbled. Mountains can do that to you, can quickly put you in your place and make human affairs seem very small and transient. It happened once again on this morning in mid-April 1997, more than three months after Police Chief Tom Koby's press conference. Spring had arrived in Colorado and last January's cold snap now seemed as distant as Koby's remarks on that brittle evening. He had made only one comment that had echoed into the future.

"The less you know," he had told the media and viewing public, "the easier it is to give advice."

This clearly meant that the authorities knew a lot more than the reporters did, but beyond that the statement was open to interpretation. Did it also mean that the police hadn't grasped the murder yet, so everyone should just relax and let the system do its work? Or that Boulder detectives had already concluded that the killing was highly complicated and going to be very difficult to solve? Or that they'd handled the investigation so badly that it was doubtful it ever could be solved? Or that, for some vague but powerful reason, they weren't committed to solving it? Or did Koby's words mean something else altogether, something impenetrable to those outside Boulder's legal system? Nearly one hundred days after the press conference, no answers had emerged.

I had driven to the Boulder County Justice Center to meet with District Attorney Alex Hunter. Several times between January and late March 1997, I had resisted the urge to pick up the phone and contact him. Finally, I sent him a fax and a week or so later he called and invited me in. Hunter was the head legal official in his county and in most circumstances would have been viewed as the leading figure dedicated to the prosecution of the Ramsey case. But these were not even close to most circumstances.

In recent weeks, I had watched Hunter on television and he had captured my attention. Many D.A.s are macho figures who like to swagger inside their authority. They conjure up cops with law degrees to put behind their badges. Hunter was soft-spoken, thoughtful, and not afraid of showing his vulnerable side in public. He seemed sensitive and unconventional, which was how the town of Boulder viewed itself. I had never met anyone in his position with quite this personality.

Since January, some media people had been regularly blasting Hunter's method of overseeing the Ramsey case, which was to proceed very carefully and cautiously. Yet it was possible that the D.A. was doing the right thing by not panicking or rushing to judgment or giving into public pressure and immediately arresting John and Patsy Ramsey—despite being pushed in that direction not just by public opinion, as expressed on talk radio, but, in a much more serious way, by the Boulder Police Department. Although the department's commander, John Eller, had never led a murder investigation before, he believed that there was no reason to suspect anyone outside the family. Nor had he aggressively sought the help of other investigative agencies more experienced in dealing with homicides; early on, he was satisfied that the case had been made.

Hunter was just the opposite. During a nationally televised news conference on February 13, 1997, seven weeks after JonBenet was killed, he had shown his flexibility and surprised virtually everyone by announcing the hiring of the two most respected members of O.J. Simpson's winning team: Barry Scheck and Dr. Henry Lee. Hunter knew that these men had been far superior in the courtroom (especially at taking apart tainted evidence) to the prosecutors who had tried Simpson, and that if the Boulder D.A.'s office had any chance of finding and convicting the girl's murderer, he was going to need some qualified help.

At his February news conference, Hunter had sounded quite optimistic when discussing the progress of the investigation:

"We're in a zone, Tom [Koby] and I. We know this case is going to be solved and we know where we're headed. But we're going to do it our way and we're willing to pay for the consequences of our actions. We know people want swift justice. We get calls about this all the time. These are the feelings and the conscience of our community, and we're sensitive to this. We've been called arrogant and unaccountable to the people of Boulder. I don't feel I'm being arrogant, but smart, and I was elected to be smart."

Then he made some rather startling comments: "I want to say something to the person or persons who committed this crime, the person or persons who took this baby from us. I mentioned the list of suspects narrows. Soon there will be no one on the list but you. When that time comes...Chief Koby and I and our people ... are going to bear down on you. You have stripped us of any mercy that we might have had in the beginning of this investigation. We will see that justice is served in this case and that you pay for what you did and we have no doubt that will happen."

On this warm spring morning, the creek behind the Boulder County Justice Center roared against its banks and sent foam into the air. Melting snow in the mountains had become, at this lower elevation, a crashing stream. As I walked into the center, the sound quickly faded. The building was strikingly calm and clean for a structure designed to deal with crime. No cigarette butts had been stamped out on these floors. No walls had been scarred by outraged shoes and no litter was visible. The halls were uncrowded and the employees who ran the metal-detection equipment near the front door were friendly. Boulder, an attractive college town of one hundred thousand affluent, highly educated people, saw very few murders; JonBenet's had been the only official homicide in the city throughout 1996. Evil things were not supposed to happen here, and certainly not to children.

A few minutes early for my appointment, I wandered out

into a courtyard, where two men were huddling over Styrofoam coffee cups. I recognized only the sixty-year-old Hunter, a smallish figure with sandy-colored hair and a thin mustache. He bore a passing resemblance to the actor/comedian Martin Mull. For almost a quarter century, Alex Hunter had been Boulder County's district attorney, and his tenure had never been quite predictable.

When initially running for office in 1972, the year in which eighteen year olds were first allowed to vote, Hunter had advocated reclassifying the possession of marijuana as a misdemeanor. During the past two decades, he had fired seven staff members for attending a holiday party that featured cocaine; had unsuccessfully tried to publish the names of drunk drivers in the newspaper; had stopped the practice of forcing rape victims to take polygraph tests; had hired a woman to investigate sex crimes; and had supported a program to distribute clean needles to addicts. He was known for being innovative, calculating, and a good listener. To get citizens' feedback, he had held many town meetings—twelve hundred in all—and had appeared on a talk radio show called "Dial the D.A." He was also known as a longtime player in local Democratic politics, once chairing the Boulder County Democratic Party (in the 1996 election, Boulder's populace had supported Bill Clinton by more than 80 percent).

Hunter's personal life had been equally unpredictable. Some ill-advised real estate investments had once caused him to declare bankruptcy. He had had four wives and had fathered five children, but for the past fourteen years, he'd been married to a gynecologist at the University of Colorado. They had an eleven-year-old daughter, Brittany, and an eight-year-old son, John.

Throughout his career, the strongest criticism leveled at Hunter was that he had dodged complicated or controversial cases. These included murder or child-abuse cases, but mostly they were crimes involving illegal narcotics. "As a drug lawyer in Boulder," a local defense attorney remarked, "it's easy to look like a genius. The D.A.'s office gives you great deals for your clients just to get rid of you."

Unlike many D.A.s, Hunter believed in crime prevention and rehabilitation more than punishment. Instead of racking up as many convictions as possible, he wanted to keep people from entering the often self-perpetuating loop of arrest, incarceration, release from prison, and re-arrest for another offense. First-time nonviolent offenders in Boulder County often received a two-year deferred sentence. Because of his willingness to make deals with defense lawyers, Hunter had been labeled the "Monty Hall of District Attorneys." He countered this image by saying that while most D.A.s plea bargained about 90 percent of their cases, his office only averaged a few points higher than that. He simply ran the legal system in the relaxed manner that was in keeping with the laidback lifestyle that Boulder promoted when recruiting new governmental projects or high-tech businesses. Every weekday, the D.A.'s office completely shut down for an hour between 12:00 and 1:00 P.M. as the wheels of justice stopped grinding for lunch.

Over the years, Hunter's attitudes about crime had generated conflict between himself and the police department.

"The cops in Boulder," says Phillip Battany, a retired Boulder Police Department officer with more than a decade on the force, "try to do their jobs, but sometimes it's impossible. Because the town has only one political party—the Democrats—everyone who's important in Boulder is allied with everyone else and the place is run like a ruling elite runs a private club. For years it was a sanctuary for drug dealers and users. There was no narcotics enforcement when I was a policeman because that's how the people in power wanted it.

It was completely haywire from a cop's point of view, and that's why I eventually quit. Nothing that goes on in town would surprise me."

In September 1997, five Boulderites died of heroin poisoning. A retired local physician named Robert McFarland spent more than a decade trying to find out why only a single individual had been prosecuted after Boulder cops had busted one of the largest heroin labs in America in the early eighties. McFarland never did receive an acceptable answer from the authorities. "The whole legal system in Boulder has produced a hands-off environment," he says, "and Alex Hunter has been the right man for the job. His people just don't take on difficult prosecutions, because it's too risky. If they don't think they can get a clear-cut victory, they back off."

Sitting with Hunter in the courtyard was a tall, aging, leathery-looking man with a husky voice. He clandestinely held a cigarette, cupping it in his palm (you're not supposed to break the antismoking law in Boulder, particularly at the Justice Center and even more particularly when you're talking with the D.A.). The tall man glanced my way, but I acted as if I weren't watching them. They huddled more closely and began to laugh among themselves. I went back inside and took a seat in the lobby of Hunter's office.

A few minutes later, the D.A. walked out to the lobby, shook my hand, and led me back into his private chambers, where I sat down on a large comfortable chair. The smoker from the courtyard joined us. He was Deputy D.A. Bill Wise, who, according to Boulder scuttlebutt, frequently had been as much in charge of things as Hunter was. Wise and Hunter had known each other since Hunter had come to Boulder at age eighteen from Briarcliff Manor, New York, to attend the

University of Colorado. After graduating from the university's law school, Hunter had clerked for a justice of the Colorado Supreme Court and a deputy D.A. in Boulder. Then he and Wise had worked together in private practice before Hunter became the district attorney.

"So that was you outside," Wise said to me.

I nodded at him. "You didn't look like you wanted to be interrupted."

"We were laughing about the media," he said with a mischievous grin.

"Really?" I asked.

"About Peter Boyles," he chuckled.

Hunter blushed and joined in.

For nearly a hundred days, Boyles had been broadcasting on his Denver radio talk show that he had no doubt about who had killed JonBenet, even if the Boulder Police Department, the D.A.'s office, the Colorado Bureau of Investigation, and the Federal Bureau of Investigation had not yet made that determination. Boyles boldly implied that the girl's parents, John and Patsy, were guilty. For the past few months he had been predicting their arrest in the next two or three days, or at the end of the week, or at the start of the following week at the latest, or . . .

Boyles came from workingclass Pittsburgh. In years past he had prominently displayed a penchant for grandstanding and a considerable chip on his shoulder toward anyone who he believed had led a more privileged life than he had. John Ramsey was a multimillionaire who ran a computer business named Access Graphics; Patsy was a former Miss America contestant; and Boulder was a middle- and upper-middle-class university town, with some undeniable pretensions. The JonBenet phenomenon presented Boyles with the opportunity he had been looking for and the chip exploded.

On the air, he liked to play the old cartoon classic, "Looney Tunes," as a musical commentary on life in Boulder, as well as a parody of the Warren Zevon rock song, "Were-wolves of London." The new number, "Werewolves of Boulder," ridiculed Hunter and Chief Koby.

Since JonBenet's death, Boyles's local ratings had jumped from fifteenth to fourth. He reached 28,000 listeners every quarter hour. On 630 AM, KHOW, he now practiced what he openly called "yellow radio," echoing the old notion of "yellow journalism," which made no attempt to be objective or fair in its coverage of people or events. Things "yellow" existed for one reason only—to skewer your targets, to slam them with impunity, and then to stand back and laugh at your handiwork. It was rabid dog radio, and as Boyles's ratings indicated, audiences found it irresistible.

"Why," I asked Hunter, "were you laughing about Boyles?"

He started to answer, but Wise cut him off.

"Now, now," the deputy D.A. said to his boss, "don't criticize the media. You'll just get in trouble."

Wise spoke from experience. A few comments from him to the press following the murder had gotten him officially bounced from the case. In an unofficial capacity, he still consulted with Hunter regularly on the homicide and in the months ahead would help build the D.A.'s connections with certain members of the media to bolster Hunter's public credibility.

The D.A. waved his hand at his longtime friend and colleague. "I'm not running for office again," he said, "and I really don't give too much of a damn what people say, but our skins are still not thick. It's tough to get pounded day after day by the talk shows."

Hunter did not sound as optimistic as he had at the

February 13 press conference, his voice conveying more exasperation than authority. He had been vacationing in Maui with his family when JonBenet had been killed, and he hadn't returned to Boulder until four days later. By then, the investigation had already become a forensic nightmare, full of police bumbling, damaged potential evidence, and infighting among the cops. Then the national media had descended on Boulder—like the invasion of locusts that had clouded the skies above the town back in 1860—and colossally magnified the detectives' mistakes.

"We just want to get at the truth," Hunter said. "Other than that, I don't have an agenda."

I glanced around his office, which held a handsome old wooden desk, rows of legal books on the shelves above us, and a picture of the deceased girl wearing a pink sweater. I was struck by the informal openness of this environment and how different it was from the atmosphere that had prevailed in Los Angeles during the Simpson case. These men displayed none of the anger, fear, vanity, or career-climbing paranoia that I saw embedded in the skins of lawyers, private investigators, journalists, and police officers in Southern California.

I felt strangely hopeful.

Wise looked straight at me and said, "The people in L.A. tried to shoehorn the evidence to nail O.J. Simpson and some of it just didn't fit. We're trying to do something different here."

My hope surged higher. Making mistakes is inevitable in law enforcement, but a far greater sin is the unwillingness to learn from the past.

Hunter opened his pen, balancing a small tablet on his lap. "Tell us what you've been looking into," he said.

2

I began describing some pictures of young girls that I had recently seen on the Internet. They were five, six, or seven years old. A few were older. They were naked and tied up and were being sexually assaulted. They were being raped. They had ropes around their hands, belts around their ankles and wrists, scarves stuffed in their mouths. The girls were laid out flat on metal tables or hanging right-side-up or upside-down from the ceiling. Several of them looked foreign, but others were American. Their pictures were being sold or traded in the global underground market for child pornography in cyberspace.

Nothing I'd yet seen or heard or read about the Ramsey case, I told Hunter and Wise, had evoked the image of the dead JonBenet—with a cord looped around her neck and another cord tied around her wrist—more than these Internet photos of very small girls being abused for someone's amusement.

Hunter had been staring at me intently and taking notes. The police, he now said cautiously, had looked into child pornography early on, taking as many as 180 videos from the Ramsey residence, but they'd found nothing linking Jon-Benet's father or anyone else in her family to this activity. "We even subpoenaed John Ramsey's personal computer files," the D.A. said, "but came up empty."

"Have you looked for pornography connections outside the family?" I asked.

"We're not there yet," Hunter said. "Our focus is still where you think it is, on the parents."

"Photographers," I said, repeating what some computer crime experts had been telling me, "are always looking for youngsters who may be rising stars as actresses or models or beauty queens. These kids make up the pool that feeds the growing appetite for child pornography. Nude pictures of little girls may be very valuable one day, if they eventually become famous."

"Everyone who knows about beauty pageants," Hunter replied, "has told us that JonBenet definitely had 'the look'—that classic, southern, blonde-haired, blue-eyed look that everyone wants. She was already a winner on the pageant circuit and she certainly had a future as a beauty queen. But you're telling us that there's a whole world attached to computerized child pornography?"

"Yes," I said. "People buy and sell and trade these images. While I was looking at the pictures, several men came online searching for risqué photos of JonBenet. One was offering pictures of his own daughter for them."

"That's very, very interesting," Hunter said. "I knew this stuff was going on, but I didn't realize how much was out there. Did you see anyone using a garotte on the Internet?"

I shook my head. "Just ropes and belts and scarves."

"Very interesting."

High-tech people associated with law enforcement—cybercops, as they are called—were going online and posing as kids willing to get involved with pedophiles. When the pedophiles made dates with these "youngsters" at a given location, the police showed up and arrested them. Cybercops, I told the men, could essentially do the same thing with child pornography: send it out and trade photos on the Net, while searching for illicit images of JonBenet or other girls.

"This is a very fertile area of investigation," I said, "but it's difficult for a journalist to get close to. If I download child pornography, I'm committing a felony."

"You don't want to do that," Hunter said, "but it's also tricky for the government to investigate this sort of thing. You can just imagine what my friends in the media would do if they heard about us sending out child porn pictures. They would go crazy."

"Oh, boy," Wise chuckled. Somebody knocked on the D.A.'s door.

"Yes?" Hunter called out.

A middle-aged woman stepped inside and apologized for interrupting our meeting. She said that the D.A.'s eleven-year-old daughter had just called, but it wasn't urgent for him to phone back.

Hunter gazed across the room at the woman. His face fell and he looked stricken.

"I know what that's about," said the man who was currently the most criticized legal official in America. "I forgot to take her clarinet to school."

The woman bowed her head.

"Thank you," Hunter said softly, and she left. He was wearing the expression of someone who had inadvertently let down one of his children.

"Well," he said, turning back to me, "we need to explore this pornographic thing more. You haven't found any pictures of JonBenet on the Internet, have you?"

"I've found many pictures of her, but they're not risqué. They're beauty pageant photos mostly. Or things that have already appeared in newspapers or magazines."

"Who do you think might have taken these other kinds of pictures of her?"

"I don't know, but this girl was in front of the camera a

lot. It's probably worth talking to some of her local photographers."

Hunter nodded. "I may speak to the FBI about this. The Internet is a federal area, and this could be important."

Wise excused himself and went outside to smoke.

I started to get up, but then hesitated, sensing that Hunter didn't want me to go immediately. Most legal authorities are distant or brusque or arrogant, especially with reporters, whom they often treat with mistrust or disdain. Hunter had a curiosity, a modesty, a gentleness that was tangible when you were sitting next to him. He had a way of making you feel welcome, as if he had time just for you, but something more than that was going on. The man who was at the very center of this entire event—the man who had been besieged by hundreds, if not thousands, of phone calls about the Ramsey murder, the man who would ultimately have to decide whether or not to file charges in the case—appeared lonely and rather confused. He appeared strikingly human.

Hunter had faced difficulties in office before. On December 26, 1982, fourteen years to the day before JonBenet's body was discovered, a three year old named Michael Manning was reported missing in Boulder County. For weeks, detectives searched for the child and the crime drew headlines across the country. Hunter appeared on TV and made an impassioned plea for information about Michael, promising amnesty in exchange for his safe return, but no one came forward. The police then promised the boy's mother, Elizabeth, that if she cooperated with them, she would be dealt with not as a suspect, but as a witness. She agreed to help and took them to her son's makeshift grave, in a mobile home park, and confessed that her boyfriend had beaten Michael to death while she'd stood by and watched.

Before hearing this confession, the detectives had failed to read Elizabeth her Miranda rights, and after murder charges were filed against her and her boyfriend, Elizabeth's crucial admission was thrown out of court. Because of the publicity the case had generated, Hunter came under intense pressure to prosecute both adults, so he did, but the mother received only a one-year sentence, while the boyfriend got a decade for assault and felony child abuse. The case did nothing to build Hunter's reputation as a successful prosecutor. More important, it made him leery of listening to public opinion and filing murder charges unless he felt certain that he could get a conviction.

As tragic as the Michael Manning case had been, it had not prepared Hunter for the challenge he was now confronting at the end of his career. Nothing had prepared him for JonBenet's murder—or for dealing with the child's mother and father in the aftermath of the crime. The D.A. was not simply trying to figure out who had killed a little girl, which was hard enough under these conditions. He was also engaged in public trench warfare with the Ramseys and their high-powered lawyers, was working with a police department that had made investigative errors, was surrounded by an ill-tempered media and an increasingly disgruntled local population, and was encountering distrust for his entire method of running the Boulder County D.A.'s office. One hundred days after the murder, he looked a bit overwhelmed.

The burden of proof for holding someone legally responsible for the child's death was not on the media's shoulders (as an old newspaperman once told me, "Editorial writers are the people who ride out of the hills after the battle is over and shoot the wounded"). The burden of spending tax dollars to investigate and prosecute one or more defendants did not lay with any of Hunter's critics. The burden of searching for and carrying out justice was on Hunter's shoulders and he had recently learned from the O.J. Simpson saga just what a burden that could be. The state of California had spent nine million dollars and taken six months to present evidence against Simpson. Then the jury freed him after less than three hours of deliberation.

Hunter created the impression of a man who wanted to close out his tenure in office by doing the right thing in the most visible criminal case in Colorado history, but the question remained: What *was* the right thing in these utterly confounding circumstances?

3

At 5:52 A.M. on December 26, 1996, Patsy Ramsey dialed 911 and reported finding a rambling, two-and-a-half-page ransom note, torn from a legal pad, at the bottom of a staircase in her Boulder home. The note said that her daughter, JonBenet, had been kidnapped by a "small foreign faction" and those holding her were demanding $118,000, to be exchanged for the girl later that day. If the money were not delivered, the child would be beheaded. Seven minutes after Patsy made the call, the police arrived at her address, a fifteen-room, 6,800-square-foot, Tudor-style residence in the upscale Chautauqua neighborhood of Boulder.

John Ramsey then phoned Fleet White, a local oil man, and some other family friends. White owned a business, Fleet Oil, which he ran from his Boulder home. The night before, which was Christmas, the Ramseys had driven a few blocks over to the Whites' home for a small, festive gathering. Around 9:30 P.M., the Ramseys had returned to their house, apparently intending to go to bed early, because at dawn they had plans to fly to their second home in Charlevoix, Michigan.

Fleet White and John Ramsey had an intense personal relationship that some people said included jealousy. Like Ramsey, White was a successful businessman, he was married, and had a six-year-old girl, Daphne, who was the same age as

JonBenet. But the Ramseys had a patina of glamour that Fleet and Priscilla White did not. In 1978, Patsy Ramsey had been crowned Miss West Virginia and then competed for the Miss America title in Atlantic City. She was outgoing and charming and did charity work for some of Boulder's most prestigious philanthropic organizations. In the past few years, she'd gone through a life-and-death battle with ovarian cancer, but after chemotherapy and other healing treatments, including large doses of prayer, she was now winning this struggle.

By age six, JonBenet had already become a child beauty queen herself, holding, among others, the titles of Little Miss Colorado, Little Miss Charlevoix, America's Royale Little Miss, and Colorado All-Star Kids Cover Girl. John Ramsey ran the highly profitable Access Graphics and had been voted Boulder's 1995 "Entrepreneur of the Year." In the twelve months just ending, Access Graphics had broken the billion-dollar sales mark for the first time, and the fifty-three-year-old Ramsey had recently celebrated this triumph by pouring champagne for several hundred of his employees at a holiday office party. Between John's accumulation of wealth and corporate power, Patsy's cancer recovery, and their daughter's growing reputation on the child pageant circuit, the Ramseys had had a great year—until right now.

Shortly after receiving Ramsey's call at dawn on December 26, 1996, Fleet White arrived at his friend's home, which was soon crowded with police officers, more family acquaintances, and the Ramseys' minister, the Reverend Rol Haverstock of St. John's Episcopal Church. When the police saw the ransom note, they assumed that JonBenet had, in fact, been kidnapped and taken from her home. Because of this, they did not empty the house of civilians and search it thoroughly.

Instead, they casually questioned the Ramseys and set about preparing to tap the phones in order to trace the expected ransom call. One of the officers, Linda Arndt, the first detective to arrive at the residence, devoted part of her morning to calming down Patsy, who was weeping uncontrollably.

Several hours passed while the police obtained a search warrant for the house and waited for the ransom call, which never came. At a few minutes past 1:00 P.M., John Ramsey decided to look through the residence himself and, with Fleet White accompanying him, headed straight down to the basement. Ramsey lodged opened the door to a small wine cellar. There on the floor, with duct tape spread across her lips and a white cord tied around her neck and wrist, lay the strangled JonBenet, with a bashed skull. Her father screamed, bent over, ripped the tape from her mouth, lifted her into his arms, and carried her upstairs, placing the corpse near the Christmas tree and, in the process, tampering with the crime scene and preventing any pristine forensic investigation of it.

When Patsy saw the body, she became hysterical, praying and screaming and asking God to raise her daughter from the dead, as He had done with Lazarus. The Ramseys' friends looked on in horror. In life, the 45-pound JonBenet had been outfitted in lavish, sequined outfits and adorned with full make up, so that she could enter and win beauty contests. Her cosmetics, elaborately teased hair, and pageant clothes, costing well into the thousands of dollars, had given her the disturbing appearance of an exotic and expensive doll that featured a woman's face, eyes, and seductive on-stage movements in a child's body. She had looked extremely knowing for her age and not quite real. Lying dead by the Christmas tree, she evoked the image of a discarded, battered toy. The sight of her caused Patsy to vomit.

* * *

Five days later, on December 31, scores of mourners filed into suburban Atlanta's Peachtree Presbyterian Church for JonBenet's funeral service. The sanctuary was decorated with poinsettias and sunlight shot through the stained-glass windows. Before the service began, grieving friends and family members lingered over the small casket, kissing JonBenet's cheeks and stroking her long, blonde hair. Then the Reverend W. Frank Harrington, who had baptized the girl and married her parents sixteen years earlier, stood and addressed the congregation.

"The mind cannot accept," he said, "and the heart refuses to grasp the death of one so young, who is suddenly taken from us by cruelty and malice by some unworthy person. When a child is lost, one feels that part of the future is gone."

The Ramseys sat in the front row, John rubbing his wife's back and young Burke, JonBenet's nine-year-old brother, restlessly kicking his feet back and forth under the pew. Reverend Harrington read a song from "Gypsy," the victim's favorite musical, and led everyone in "Jesus Loves Me, This I Know," whose childlike lyrics and simple melody caused sobs to reverberate throughout the church.

When the service was over, Patsy walked up to the coffin and lowered her veiled face. She placed her arms around the casket, holding on and swaying, until her husband slowly led her away. JonBenet was taken to a cemetery near the St. James Episcopal Church, her grave shadowed by a dogwood tree. She was buried wearing a pageant dress and the tiny crown she had recently won in the Colorado Little Miss Christmas contest. As these events were unfolding in Atlanta, half a continent away in Boulder people were dropping off stuffed animals and other toys in front of the Ramsey home. They had tied ribbons to the holiday candy canes that aligned the sidewalk and erected a cross on the lawn. A message scrawled across it read that the mourners would see the girl in heaven.

The day after the funeral—January 1, 1997—John and Patsy appeared on the CNN cable-TV network and proclaimed their innocence to a captivated nationwide audience, while offering a $50,000 reward for information leading to the arrest of JonBenet's killer. John Ramsey appeared fairly normal on TV, if a bit strained around the eyes and mouth. He looked like a corporate executive trained in crisis management who was trying to cope with a very tough public relations problem. Almost from the moment the body had been discovered, he had followed the advice of Mike Bynum, a lawyer-friend in Boulder, and began putting together an expensive legal team to protect himself and his wife from any activities or allegations on the part of the Boulder police or legal system.

He told CNN that since December 26, he and Patsy had been cooperating with the police. They had, in fact, given hair, blood, and handwriting samples to the authorities, but had not yet appeared at a formal interview with them. John said they had shared all their thoughts with the detectives about who may have committed the crime, but for now, "We have no answer."

Patsy sat beside him, looking dreadful. She had the half-open eyes of someone who had been crying nonstop and taking sedatives; indeed, she'd consumed a possibly dangerous amount of Valium in the past few days. If she didn't seem fully conscious or aware of herself on television, she did convey more emotion than her husband. She called JonBenet "daddy's girl" and referred to her Boulder home as a "hell-hole," vowing never to live there again (the Ramseys left their house on the evening of December 26 and moved from one friend's residence to another, unable to walk the streets of Boulder without being stormed by the media; they would continue this pattern for the next several months before fleeing to Atlanta).

"There is a killer on the loose," Patsy told CNN. "We don't know who it is or if it is a he or a she. But if I were a resident of Boulder, I would tell my friends to keep your babies close to you."

These remarks would not go down well in the town where Patsy had lived since 1992. Boulder was nothing if not image conscious, and the molestation and murder of a little girl inside its city limits was not the sort of image the community wanted to promote. On January 2, a municipal spokeswoman, Leslie Aaholm, fired back at Patsy, publicly denying her contentions. Boulder did not, Aaholm insisted, have a murderer running in the streets, and other parents of small children had nothing to fear. The implication, of course, was that the killer was not at large, but had come from inside the Ramseys' home.

Aaholm was not Boulder's only official who distanced herself from the family. During Patsy's recent bout with cancer, she had become acquainted with Leslie Durgin, the town's mayor, who was also recovering from the illness. Both women were part of the local establishment and were friendly with one another, but after the murder, Mayor Durgin offered no support to the Ramseys, and neither did anyone else inside the Boulder power structure. The family was shunned.

Some people inside that power structure not only knew the Ramseys, but had visited their home only two days before the crime, when John and Patsy had held a Christmas party with dozens of guests (an unexplained 911 call from the Ramsey residence to the police had occurred during this event). It had never been revealed who had attended this gathering or if any of these friends had possessed some of the ten to fifteen sets of keys to the Ramsey house that were reportedly floating around Boulder. The guest list remained a mystery.

The Boulder establishment tacitly went along with the media's growing speculation that the Ramseys had sexually abused and killed their child and then had written the ransom note to cover up the crime. Their response to the homicide lent credence to the obvious questions: Who else could have done it? Who else but John or Patsy could have known that John's bonus at Access Graphics for 1995 was almost $118,000—the same amount as the ransom demand? Who else would have signed the note *Victory! S.B. T.C.,* which must have stood for the Subic Bay Training Center, where John Ramsey had been stationed in the Philippines in 1968 and 1969? Who else would have taken the time to write a full two and a half pages, unless it were someone living in the house who did not need to escape?

There were only four known people in the residence that night—John, Patsy, their nine-year-old son, Burke, and Jon-Benet. Most commentators reasoned that Burke could not have built a garotte, carried out such a gruesome crime alone, or penned the detailed note. There were no definitive signs of forced entry into the home and no definitively fresh foot-prints in the dusting of snow in the Ramseys' yard. In addition, the Ramseys had refused to sit down individually with the police at a formal interrogation. Didn't that right there make them guilty?

A hundred days later, the district attorney was not sure.

"JonBenet's parents," Hunter said, as we sat together in his office, "have done almost nothing to help us figure this thing out. Why would innocent people act that way?"

"I don't know," I replied.

"They obviously don't trust the cops or me. They may feel a lot of guilt over the girl's death and this has made them even quieter and more afraid. I think Patsy feels guilty about dressing JonBenet up in a grown woman's clothes and putting her in those beauty pageants. I can understand how she would feel that way."

He made some more remarks about the quality of people that the Ramseys seemed to be, while I remained silent, very taken by the fact that Hunter was thinking through his conundrum with a virtual stranger—and a journalist at that. The rest of the world may have been staring at the surface of the crime and jumping to conclusions, but the D.A. appeared to be attempting something else: He was drawing on his life-long experience as a prosecutor, a man, a husband, and a father in order to understand what he was confronting. He was utilizing his common sense and his deep political instincts.

One of the most powerful rumors early in the case was that semen was found on JonBenet's body, along with reports that she had had chronic irritation of the vaginal tissues and had been penetrated. Even though the penetration could have been done by someone outside the Ramsey family, by some foreign object, or by the child herself, many people instantly decided that the child had been molested by her father (JonBenet's bedroom was on the second floor of her spacious home, a considerable distance away from her parents' bedroom on the third floor). In March 1997, such gossip inspired Paul Hidalgo, a twenty-one-year-old student at the University of Colorado's Boulder campus, to create what was very loosely described as a "work of art," by arranging three photographs of JonBenet on a wall at the school. DADDY'S LITTLE HOOKER, he wrote next to them, and the media scrambled to the wall and sent this image around the globe.

The pictures and words set off a great stir. Callers to Denver's radio stations were delighted that someone with courage and vision had finally come forward and told the truth about John Ramsey. He was an incestuous, homicidal parent who had molested and asphyxiated his daughter. This was clear by the way he sat in a chair on television or moved his head or shifted his eyes. His body language told us that he was a sexual predator and a murderer.

"I've heard," I said carefully to Hunter, "that there was semen on JonBenet."

He immediately shook his head and replied, "There isn't any."

So much for that rumor.

In recent months, because the authorities had not been able to find any evidence that John Ramsey was a child molester, a pornographer, or that he had any criminal leanings whatsoever, the media's speculation had begun to shift toward Patsy. She had killed the child because JonBenet had a bed-wetting problem that had finally pushed her mother beyond her limits. Or because Patsy had just completed chemotherapy treatments for stage-four ovarian cancer, which has a mortality rate of 95 percent, that had left her irrational and violently out of control. Or because Patsy, who kept an open Bible near her bed, was a religious fanatic who had sacrificed her daughter on Christmas night as a kind of twisted gift to the Lord.

During the past few years, I had written three books about women who had killed. In each case, not only dress rehearsals—in which the perpetrators were not quite able to bring themselves to commit the final act—but also disruptive behaviors and a buildup to violence had preceded the slay-ings. None of these elements seemed to apply in JonBenet's murder. In the past one hundred days, and continuing throughout the coming several hundred more, not one person had emerged with a single anecdote suggesting parental abuse or anything resembling deviant activity. In fact, those who had come forward had stated the opposite: The Ramseys were a good family who loved their children. If that were true, how could there be a motiveless crime?

I looked at Hunter and brought up something I had been thinking about since January. "Was it possible that a kind of game was being played with JonBenet and that the garotte around her neck was accidentially tightened just a little too much?"

"No," he said. "This was no accident, and it was not a superficial wound on her neck. The garotte left impressions in her flesh. Whoever did this was very strong and intended to harm her. It was a vicious act."

I held my silence as he stared off into the distance.

"Somebody at a photo shoot," he said, "may have asked JonBenet to take off her clothes and she said she was going to tell her mommy. That would have been trouble. I need to look into this Internet business."

I nodded.

"Can you learn more about it?" he said.

"The Internet?"

"Yes."

I thought this was an unusual request, but I told him I would see what I could do.

"If you find out anything," Hunter said, walking me to the door, "let us know right away."

We shook hands and he thanked me for coming in. As I was leaving, he dropped a remark that underscored the entire case—and revealed the depths of his dilemma. The Boulder police had failed to treat the Ramsey home as a crime scene; failed to accept assistance from the far-more-experienced Denver Police Department, which handles roughly a hundred homicides a year, compared to Boulder's one or two; failed to employ the expertise of the mobile crime lab of the Colorado Bureau of Investigation; and failed to consider John and Patsy Ramsey as suspects.

If Commander John Eller had never supervised a murder investigation before, neither had Police Chief Tom Koby, who had learned his trade working robberies down in Houston. The FBI had eventually arrived at the Ramsey home and offered help, but not in time to prevent John Ramsey and Fleet White from finding the body and altering the evidence in the basement.

"I'm not going to give your information to the cops right away," Hunter said, as we stood in the doorway, "because I don't want them to screw it up."

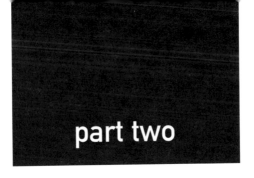

part two

Lost in Cyberspace

4

A few days after meeting with Hunter, I was in a room in Denver with some people who were sitting in front of a computer terminal. When one of them pushed a key, an advertisement for celebrity nudes came up on the screen. This service promised, for $49.95 a month, to undress many well-known people in America, including models, supermodels, actresses, television stars, and those who appeared in TV commercials. Someone pushed another key and pulled up the listings for erotic newsgroups, including those for senior citizens, Latinos, redheads, fitness buffs, and cowgirls.

"You can make an easy extra hundred grand a year on the side selling porn," a man at the terminal said. "It's almost pure profit."

He typed out "JonBenet." The dead girl was all over the Net. There were JonBenet newsgroups, chat rooms, articles, videos, photos, and volumes of e-mail about her murder. She was everywhere—as alive in cyberspace as she had once been as a youngster playing in her backyard in Boulder.

The Net displayed many of the same images as those with which the American media had lately been saturating the public: JonBenet in bathing suits, in beauty-pageant regalia, and in other costumes. There were pictures of her dressed like a sailor and a coy Little Red Riding Hood. In one pageant video, she was clad as a cowgirl, warbling offkey "I Wanna Be a Cowboy's Sweetheart." In another, she was gussied up as a Las Vegas showgirl, wearing sequins and feathers and waving her derriere in our faces. In one photograph, she was vamping in a tight black leotard, her skirt flung over her shoulder, her hand placed provocatively on her thigh, and her feet and ankles tied with black straps. In another, she wore bright red lipstick and a white dress, imitating the signature style of America's greatest sexual icon. A large button on this outfit read, *Hello, I'm Marilyn Monroe.*

The Ramsey case was pervaded with a maddening double standard, and these images of the child were no exception. They constantly appeared on the TV screen, while the news commentators condemned them. Into every living room in the nation was thrust the Great American Titillation Dilemma, whose message now could not have been more mixed: eros was fabulous for TV ratings and countless other business promotions, yet it raised uncomfortable questions. We loudly proclaimed the Ramseys' guilt (and our own innocence), while we became voyeurs, addicted to a powerful combination of sex and death, and no matter how hard we tried to rationalize our viewing, it felt unhealthy.

One could only imagine the shock JonBenet's parents experienced watching these essentially private pictures and videos become part of the worldwide visual consciousness (and as people close to the Ramseys who owned the photos began selling them to media outlets). Many of these images had come from JonBenet's involvement in beauty pageants, which had begun innocently enough, partly to help Patsy take her mind off cancer, partly because she was carrying on a family tradition begun by her maternal grandmother, Nedra Paugh, who had pushed her own daughters, Patsy and Pam, into the pageant scene when they were teenagers (JonBenet started at four), and partly because she just took to this realm.

JonBenet loved to dress up and change clothes. She loved the glory that came with performing in front of adults and winning awards, easily defeating many other contestants. She enjoyed, as most children do, the notion of acting like a grownup and moving further into the large, strange world. Meeting new people at pageants in Colorado, Michigan, and Georgia, she was learning how to be poised onstage, to draw attention to herself, and to please others. She also loved the camera and by age five had developed a definite relationship with photography. She knew how to mug, to be coy, to flirt, and to play to the lens as if it were a live audience. No wonder she kept winning more titles and was gaining a reputation on the pageant scene. Her mother—a former Miss West Virginia, after all—was too.

Child beauty pageants have a distinct class aura. They can be to the workingclass child what soccer is to the middleclass—the activity of choice. Little tribes, made up mostly of women, follow them around and promote their daughters. All across America, the same parents, grandparents, and girls meet on the weekends at malls or other venues and compete for cash and prizes. The Ramseys were anything but workingclass and their mere presence at Colorado's pageants—with Patsy's money and JonBenet's looks—gave the events a certain prestige. As a stage mother, Patsy Ramsey was a gracious winner and an even more gracious loser, offering high praise to whomever got the prize. But that was part of the pageant tradition: You smiled and hugged your opponent right after she'd defeated you.

The man at the computer downloaded some old Jon-Benet e-mail.

"Child molestation is a secret crime," one message read.

"It was Christmas night and . . . maybe Daddy had a little too much Christmas cheer to be thinking clearly."

"Get working," read another, "on the theory that Mommy did it and Daddy knows why."

"The father is the killer," read a third. "If he molested JonBenet, then he also molested his oldest daughter [Elizabeth, who had died in a car wreck in Chicago in the early nineties]. She must have committed suicide in that car because of her shame. The police know this, but aren't ready to release it."

Someone in the room said, "This kid has become an obsession with us."

"An industry," somebody else replied.

The man pushed more keys and began searching for risqué pictures of JonBenet. He sent out a message saying that he was looking for anyone with illicit photos of the dead child, and within minutes, three people replied. They were also seeking these images, and in exchange for them, they were willing to sell porn of their own. One was offering pictures of his children in return.

The man at the keyboard moved on, scrolling through the listings of one newsgroup, Incest, and another, Pedophiles. A new message came in asking us for photos of women being "gutted or roasted." I recalled a magazine article I had recently read about adult females who go online to explore their fantasies in chat rooms and are often shocked when men want to conduct a virtual gang rape of them—or even a virtual murder.

In the March/April 1997 issue of *Ms.* magazine, Debra Michaels had written an article describing the trauma experienced by women who received this graphic sexual violence on the Net. "While many may turn off their computers and leave a chat area if they feel attacked," she wrote, "they often have trouble shaking the memory that a stranger at a far-off computer terminal wanted to hurt them."

In some cases, the hurt would not be only virtual. In October 1996, a Maryland woman was found murdered behind the home of a man she had met online. In spring 1997, Jeremy Strohmeyer, an eighteen-year-old alleged devotee of Internet child pornography, followed a seven-year-old girl into a Las Vegas casino restroom, then raped and murdered her while her father gambled.

"The Internet," someone had recently told me, "is basically lawless. It's the wild, wild West all over again."

By the mid-nineties, the Net held an estimated five thousand child porn sites worldwide—with everything from still photographs and videos of children (or adults and children) engaged in sexual activity to cameras capturing and transmitting pedophilic acts in real time. Through this new technology, child molesters were now intimately connected to one another not just locally, but in different cities and even different nations around the globe. The result was something startlingly novel and problematical for law enforcement.

For one thing, it is often extremely difficult to track on the Net where such images are coming from or going, but beyond the technical challenges for cybercops lay something else. Pedophilia has always been regarded as a taboo, perhaps the very deepest taboo in modern societies. Because of this, it has been kept at the most private and secretive levels of individual sexual predation. People haven't talked about engaging in such a thing with small children in public for all the obvious reasons: It is illegal and can very quickly get one arrested.

The Internet has changed all that. Out there in cyberspace, where almost everybody uses a fake name or a fake identity and one can do just about anything while maintaining complete anonymity, people with the same sexual proclivities naturally find one another. Instead of being ashamed of seducing children, they effectively become part of a support group that encourages their behavior. Even those who had fought against their own hidden desires and stifled some of their impulses now have found it more difficult to resist temptation. Most pedophiles are repeat offenders to begin with, committing an average of thirty illicit acts before they are caught. The Net pushes them to indulge even more.

There are chat groups that advise child molesters on how to get kids away from parents; on what techniques to use to get the children to do what you want; and on the best way of conducting this kind of business without getting caught. A new criminal frontier has exploded—before law enforcement has even been able to begin to catch up with it—a frontier with no territorial boundaries.

In a 1996 scandal in Belgium, several children were killed, and the authorities tried unsuccessfully to cover up their murders, fearing the crimes would expose the pornography ring that was linked to the homicides. In 1997, another child porn scandal erupted in Spain, while in France 250 people were arrested for selling or possessing videotapes of small children being raped and tortured.

In 1998, Dutch police uncovered a group of child pornography traders in Zandvoort who were peddling images of kids—and even infants—on the Internet to residents of Russia, Great Britain, Europe, Israel, and the United States. An unnamed psychologist acting as a police consultant on the case told *The New York Times,* "For professional reasons, I have seen a lot of porn, but this left me speechless. It looks like the perpetrators are not dealing with human beings but with objects."

* * *

By 1997, police departments and antiporn groups throughout the United States were scrambling to develop strategies to fight back. Following through with Alex Hunter's request to investigate a possible link between the Ramsey murder and child pornography, I spoke with representatives of Enough Is Enough and the National Law Center for Children about the connections between pornography and the Internet. These two organizations, based in Fairfax, Virginia, provide information to parents, teachers, and government employees about the dangers of child pornography, while backing legislation to control it.

"The Department of Justice," said Bob Flores, the senior counsel for the National Law Center for Children, "is on record saying that child pornography is a growing problem for our kids. We're seeing it everywhere now. There's a kind of feeder system that keeps it going, especially among aspiring fashion models and actresses. You promise them modeling or acting jobs and get them to take off their clothes. Then you sell these pictures instead of, or in addition to, the legitimate ones. In the United States, it's a problem, but in some foreign countries, it can be much worse. Women and children sometimes end up as little more than sexual slaves.

"We'd pretty much eradicated pornography in the mails, but the Internet makes it much harder to catch the perpetrator. That's why you're seeing these markets skyrocketing all over the planet. You have Americans and other wealthy people who travel the globe and take pictures of young children, both for their own pleasure and to sell to others. Maybe they used to shoot beautiful scenery when they went abroad, because transporting pornography was risky. Now they can transfer these pictures onto the Internet very easily with digital cameras, with very little danger of being caught, so there's more and more material out there. Once it's on the Net, you can instantly send it anywhere on earth that has compatible technology. You can make a significant profit in child porn with almost no investment."

Enough Is Enough has sent out literature that describes hard-core pornography as a billion-dollar-a-year industry that threatens our children "both morally and physically.... Any child with a computer and a modem can simply 'call up' and . . . 'print out' pictures that are unspeakably pornographic." It also describes how child predators use the Internet to make contact with children, then meet and molest them. "There are more outlets for hard-core pornography in America than McDonald's restaurants."

At the western edge of Denver in the suburb of Lakewood, one of the state's leading computer crime experts, Chuck Davis of the Colorado Bureau of Investigation, explained to me that Internet pornography now represents one-quarter to one-half of the entire porn business.

"Child porn is the largest growing computer crime," he said. "I've seen these crimes being committed in half-million-dollar homes and in trailer parks. The crooks are very bold, because they don't feel they'll get caught. The authorities are reluctant to pursue these cases, because mayors and state legislators and other politicians want fast results. Child porn investigations take time if you want to put together a good case. Only the stupid people are now being tracked and arrested for these offenses.

"Is organized crime a part of this business? I'd be extremely surprised if it wasn't. We haven't yet found the people who really bankroll this stuff, because we haven't gone far enough up the food chain to see who's running it."

I asked him if he had ever looked for or seen any illicit pictures of JonBenet in cyberspace.

"I've seen many pictures of her on the Internet—beauty pageant photos and family shots—but I haven't searched for anything else, because no one has asked me to. There are rumors about big photography outlets distributing child porn now, but who knows? Nothing would surprise me. What is easier than taking pictures of children and selling them?"

On a spring evening in downtown Denver, I sat with a man in an uncrowded coffeeshop who had once worked in the pornography business.

"You got a lot of action now in the adult and child porn markets," he said, sipping a cup of tea. "You can make money selling pictures, but you can also make money over time on the inflation of your negatives. It's like a long-term investment. The more famous a person becomes, the more valuable their image gets. If you take a picture of someone when they're nine or ten, and they get famous at fifteen or twenty or twenty-five, your photos will really appreciate. The challenge is to find some chick with a certain look and place a long-range bet on her negative. In five years, maybe the tabloids or *Penthouse* or *Playboy* will pay you a bundle for it."

He sipped his tea and continued, "Porn is like any retail business. You got tiered markets for different audiences. You got mass-market photos that everyone wants. They aren't worth that much. You got more explicit photos that only collectors would be interested in. And you got the good, expensive stuff for the freakier slice of the market. You can create limited editions of prints of nude celebrities and jack up the price this way. Supply and demand. Like selling baseball cards.

"Fetishes make the marketplace run. They fuel the desires, and then you create the products that satisfy those desires. The more twisted the desire, the more the product costs. An image of someone's face is worth X. Her body is worth three X. Her body doing certain things is worth five X. Then maybe ten X. Like in any subculture, there's a certain kinky underground prestige in collecting the weirdest material.

"The Internet has opened up whole new markets in the U.S. and abroad. The pie is getting bigger. You can take pictures with digital cameras now and transfer them right onto the Net. You can also fake a lot of things, by putting famous people's heads on someone else's body. There are scams everywhere, and great business opportunities for photographers. A lot of them are only in it for the money and don't care what they're shooting. It's like talking to strippers in the clubs. In real life, they're getting nurse's degrees at the local college, but nude dancing pays their tuition."

5

The Boulder County Jail sits on a rise east of town—a modern-looking structure evoking a big erector set. At 4:45 one spring afternoon, I parked the car in the rain, ran inside, emptied my pockets, and took a chair in the lobby next to some Mexican women and girls. Two of them held babies and one woman had a bruise along her chin. They huddled together, speaking Spanish and glancing at me as if I were a cop. On the lobby phone, a blonde bondswoman, wearing sharp high heels and a black leather jacket and smelling of fresh bourbon, twirled an unlit cigarette. She looked as though she would be very difficult to surprise.

At exactly 5:00 P.M., a prison bureaucrat told us to form a line by the metal detector leading into the visitors' room. Because my boots had nails in the soles, I had to take them off and toss them through the electronic doorway before I was admitted. While we waited in a crowded anteroom, guards marched the inmates out of their cells and into a large open room. In front of us, a thick iron door buzzed opened and we moved toward the prisoners. I searched their faces, mostly young and dark, until a middle-aged pair of eyes caught mine. The man smiled at me. I was oddly moved, raising my hand and smiling back, feeling unnerved and childlike, as I always feel in prisons.

The man approached and pumped my hand. He smelled of sweat, a too-sweet odor—like snuff—and perhaps old semen. We found a couple of chairs and sat down facing each other. While describing his past at length, he asked me to scoot closer and speak very softly. I did, anxious to hear what he could tell me about child pornography in the area.

"How did you hear about me?" he said.

"Someone in Denver said you know about child porn. Do you?"

He shrugged and looked at the floor. He glanced at the younger men sitting near us, tightly clustered with their wives and girlfriends and children. He studied the guards in the corners, their hands on their hips, their eyes on the big clock on the wall. He leaned toward me and whispered, "I have some names and connections. Some people in Boulder are into the child stuff."

"Is John Ramsey one of them?"

"No. I never heard of him before all this happened."

"Then who?"

"I can't help you."

"Why not?" He had needy, ferretlike eyes. He had encrustations on his lips, and his fingernails were black.

"There are names . . . around town," he said.

"Just men?"

"And a couple of women."

"They sell and trade pornography?"

"Yes."

"On the Internet?"

"That's part of it."

I dropped a prominent Boulder name.

His head popped up. "How do you know that?"

"Were you involved with them?"

"No. I just stole things from people. I really needed the money and—"

A guard slapped a Formica-topped table with his palm, cracking the air.

"Time to go!" he said.

I glanced at the clock: thirty minutes had disappeared.

The women visitors began to stand, but the men grabbed at their arms and hands, pulling them back down. The women smiled and twisted away, gently trying to free themselves.

"Let's go!" the guard said, hitting the table again.

Slowly, reluctantly, the inmates released their grips and the women back pedalled toward the anteroom, waving and holding up their babies.

The man next to me stood up.

"Is there more?" I asked him.

"Yes. Come back, okay?"

I nodded, rising and offering my hand. He took it and squinted his eyes, as if emotion were gathering there, so I turned and walked toward the door.

When I got home that evening, there was a phone message from Jeffrey Shapiro. A would-be journalist living in South Florida, he had first contacted me the previous December, after reading something I'd written. Twenty-three years old and still living with his parents, he was fantastically eager to start a career in journalism and thought I might be able to help him. He had brazenly proposed flying to Denver, moving into my basement, and freelancing from there. Our discussion of this option had been very brief.

In the following weeks, he had tried unsuccessfully to hook on with the *Miami Herald* before turning to something that was more available, more lucrative, and no doubt more fun—something that required a sense of adventure, if no real experience as a reporter. An uncle landed him an interview with the *Globe,* a national tabloid, and he was given the opportunity to work freelance for them. He was immediately sent to Boulder to cover the hottest tabloid story since the O.J. Simpson case—the death of JonBenet Ramsey. Shapiro's assignment in Boulder was clear: Do absolutely *anything* to generate articles, but stay out of jail. As a *Globe* senior executive told him, "Develop sources and uncover fresh information, but don't break the law. Go right up to the line, but don't ever cross it." The *Globe* started him at $150 a day (his life savings at the moment was $50), and gave him a late-model car and an apartment in Boulder, plus other expense money. The young man had not only escaped his mother and father—he had landed in tabloid heaven.

In its coverage of the Ramsey case, the *Globe* had a very conscious marketing strategy. The editors of the *National Enquirer* tabloid, whose circulation was approaching five million, had discovered a bonanza in covering the O.J. Simpson case. The *Globe,* which sold only 1.3 million copies a week, had been looking for a similar opportunity to bolster its circulation. When Boulder's little beauty queen was found strangled to death in her wealthy parents' basement on the day after Christmas 1996—a tabloid headline if there ever was one—the *Globe* was ready. In January 1997, the paper made headlines by purchasing and publishing photos of the crime. It had hit the motherlode and was soon running fast and hard with the contention from "sources close to the investigation" that JonBenet's parents were involved in child abuse and murder.

Before long, Tony Frost, the tabloid's editor, had appeared on *Larry King Live,* Geraldo Rivera's daytime TV program, and other media venues, debating the notion of the Ramseys' culpability. By virtue of these appearances, he soon became one of the leading "experts" on the case. His paper kept Jon-Benet on the front page of forty-six out of fifty-two issues, and the *Globe* received more mail on this subject than on any other in its forty-four-year history. Meanwhile, the *National Enquirer* was hardly ignoring the murder: The homicide was featured on thirty-eight of forty of its covers. In order to keep up with the tabloids, mainstream celebrity gossip columnists, like Cindy Adams, also appeared on the talk shows and implied that the Ramseys were guilty.

In March 1997, onto the front lines of this tabloid warfare strolled Jeff Shapiro, ready and willing for combat. He wore aviator shades, Doc Martens shoes, and an army jacket. He immediately bought an $800 high-security briefcase. He was so happy to be away from home and in a town with more than ten thousand co-eds that he glided when he walked. He had daring, boundless energy, and . . . imagination.

After arriving in Boulder, he rented a car and slapped in a Metallica tape, cranking up the volume. He drove straight to the Ramseys' church, the stately St. John's Episcopal in the heart of old downtown. He cornered one of the priests, explaining that because he—Shapiro—and Jesus Christ were both political revolutionaries, he had decided to give up his Judaic birthright and convert. He wanted instruction in the basic tenets of Christianity. The priest was flattered and agreed to teach him the way to salvation. Once inside the church, however, Shapiro planned to squeeze all the tawdry Ramsey family secrets out of the good fathers and their congregation. For forty-eight hours, St. John's bought his story until another tabloid reporter working for a rival paper blew Shapiro's cover and he was drummed out of the sanctuary.

Undaunted, Shapiro approached John Andrew Ramsey, JonBenet's twenty-year-old stepbrother, in a local tavern and tried to interview him. John Andrew thought he was a stalker and called the police. Shapiro then attempted to bed one of John Andrew's ex-girlfriends, looking for a scoop. Midnights, you could find the young reporter peering into homes with binoculars and searching for clues in the trash cans of people who had housed the Ramseys in the months after the murder. You could find him climbing the trees in the Ramsey's side-yard in order to peek inside empty rooms, or using his police scanner to pick up intimate conversations in the neighbor-hood. Within a week of hitting town, he had rushed the Boulder County District Attorney Alex Hunter in a parking lot and engaged the D.A. in a conversation about the case.

Shapiro represented the latest trend in American journal-ism: tabloid aggression and agenda reporting. After watching him work for a while, I felt very old, extremely outdated, and seriously overmatched.

"Yo, dude," he said to me that evening, when I returned his phone call.

"What's up?" I asked, never quite prepared for his answer.

"I got caught yesterday trying to jump onto the roof of the Ramseys' house. Two cops busted me. It was awesome, like *Mission: Impossible.* I wanted to swing over and land on top of the house. Maybe even sneak in and roam around the rooms. How cool would it be to get down into that basement where the kid was found? I'll get in there before anyone else does."

"Were you arrested?"

"No. They just threatened me with trespassing and gave me a warning. I've got an important question for you."

"Yeah?"

"There's this chick who works for Channel 9. A reporter on the case. Older. Kind of a dirty blonde. You know her?"

"Not really."

"She's pretty hot, bro'. I think she likes me because she asked me a lot of questions yesterday. She wanted to know what I saw from the trees in their backyard. I'm getting very close to this case and she was really impressed with what I've done."

"Huh."

"I found a piece of stick on the Ramsey property. It looks just like the wooden part of the garotte that was wrapped around JonBenet's neck. I also found a piece of string tied to one of the trees. It looks just like the cord that was on the garotte. I'm gonna break this case wide open, man. I'm gonna prove that her parents killed her. Her mother did it. I'm gonna get Patsy Ramsey locked up and when I do, I'm gonna be rich and famous and on every talk show in America."

"What evidence do you have that the mother did it?"

"I just know she's guilty. I've been around women like her. My mother's a little bit like that. A lot of these women look normal, but underneath everything, they're psycho. The cops are startin' to tell me the same thing. I'm gonna help them nail her."

I liked Shapiro and occasionally I learned things from him. He had intelligence, a sense of humor, some real reportorial instincts, and he was fearless, perhaps to a fault. But at the moment, I was struggling with the impulse to lecture him about all the assumptions he was making, about the presumption of innocence in the American criminal justice system, and about drawing conclusions about Patsy Ramsey based upon his feelings for his own mother. And yet, he was merely aping what many others were saying: Patsy Ramsey was a killer and everyone knew it.

Beyond all the legal and journalistic considerations, I felt something else, which was personal and had to do with being the father of a three-year-old child. Ever since JonBenet had been murdered, I was awakening at around 2:00 A.M. and then going into my son's bedroom and standing near him, making certain that he was warmly tucked in through the wintry Colorado nights. Each time I performed this ritual, I thought about the dead Ramsey girl and listened closely for my son to draw his next breath. Once I had heard him do that, I could relax and go back to sleep.

From time to time, I tried to imagine what it was like to lose a small child, to have him or her suddenly taken by death, and to know—to feel—that his or her life would never be lived. I really could not imagine this, but whenever I made the attempt, an aching, hollow sensation would come into my chest, a sorrow without any borders or limitations. It was simply the worst thing I could conceive of, much worse than the thought of my own death.

It was impossible, of course, for someone like Shapiro, who had never raised a child, to understand these things or to grasp what took place, both physically and emotionally, between a parent and a youngster in the first five years of his or her life. It was impossible to convey the experience of holding, feeding, cleaning, nurturing, bathing, playing with, and loving a new person unless one had done those things him- or herself. Being with a child alters the nature of one's existence and one's sense of self. For many people, it opens up the portals of caring and connecting that nothing else can. It forever changes the heart.

It followed, then, that I could not explain to Shapiro how it would feel to be publicly accused of taking away that child's life—before anyone knew the facts of the matter. Or to be accused of this by hundreds or thousands or millions of people who, although they had never met the accused and knew nothing about his or her past or relationship with the child, nevertheless had no compunction whatsoever about making public accusations that he or she had done the most terrible thing an adult could do. Or to have to explain to another child—in this case, to nine-year-old Burke Ramsey—why all of those people were saying that his parents had killed his sister.

I had the urge to tell Shapiro that before he made or wrote such allegations about a mother and her daughter, he had damn well better have some evidence to back it up; that the only evidence revealed in the case thus far was a ransom note and the garotte found around the child's neck; and that the identity of the killer was still a mystery.

But I swallowed my words and let the impulse pass. What difference would my lecture make to him? My personal thoughts and feelings seemed quaint and sentimental in the social atmosphere of 1997 America. Who cared anymore about skepticism or self-restraint? Shapiro was doing exactly what the *Globe* was paying him to do and had already succeeded in Boulder beyond his wildest hopes. Did anyone in his journalistic organization or many others want to hear about the intricacies of the human heart or to consider that they could be wrong and might be causing damage that could never be undone?

"Look," I said instead. "Let me give you one piece of advice. Don't close your mind to the idea that you can be surprised by this case. It may be more complicated than you realize."

"The cops know she did it. They've already told me that."

"Don't believe everything the police say. Cops can be tricky."

"They tell me the truth," he said.

"How do you know that?"

"I just do. I've got a call coming in from headquarters. Later, dude."

6

In late April, while I was trying to learn more about Internet pornography, Hunter himself and the Boulder police were battling with the Ramseys' legal team over obtaining a formal interview with the parents. Some people thought the authorities were badly outgunned.

Within hours after the discovery of JonBenet's body, as detectives began hauling 250 items out of the Ramseys' home and booking them as potential evidence, a local attorney named Mike Bynum advised John Ramsey to get counsel at once. Ramsey quickly hired four lawyers from the respected and potent Denver firm of Haddon Morgan and Foreman. Like Hunter, Hal Haddon was a longtime player in local Democratic politics. He had orchestrated Gary Hart's first successful bid to become a United States senator from Colorado. Haddon's arrival on the case instantly threw an extra charge into an already loaded atmosphere. Haddon and Hunter knew one another. Both men had been major forces in the area's Democratic party machine. Haddon seemed to relish publicly taking on a district attorney from a smaller city—and one with a reputation for ducking controversy and difficult prosecutions. He would show Hunter no mercy.

Two lawyers from Haddon's firm, Patrick Burke and Patrick Furman, would represent Patsy Ramsey, while the other two, Lee Foreman and Bryan Morgan, would counsel her husband. This unusual maneuver of dividing up the attorneys only added to the questions circulating about the Ramseys' defense. Why did they need so many lawyers, if they really had nothing to hide? Why did they hire different sets of counsel, with one pair for the mother and another for the father? What strategy did this indicate they were planning? And how much were they paying all these people?

The answer to the first query came quickly. On December 28, 1996, John Meyer, Boulder County's coroner, finished his examination of JonBenet's body and completed his autopsy report, which would remain sealed for months. The police, in an unorthodox move that clearly revealed their suspicions about the murder, asked Meyer not to return the body to the parents—who were preparing to hold a memorial service in Boulder on December 29 and the burial in Atlanta two days later—but instead to hold onto the corpse until the Ramseys had completed a lengthy interrogation with detectives. John and Patsy Ramsey, it was now obvious, needed a good lawyer just so that they could lay their daughter to rest. The Ramseys, led by their indignant band of attorneys, were prepared to fight this issue in court, but the police backed down and gave JonBenet back to her family.

If hiring four lawyers made the couple look guiltier in many people's eyes, then the expansion of their legal team unleashed even more speculation. The services of two Denver private investigative firms, H. David Williams's and Ellis Armistead's, were enlisted at approximately $100 an hour apiece; John Douglas, a criminal profiler who had worked for the F.B.I., was hired at around $200 an hour; two unnamed handwriting experts were brought in to examine the ransom note at roughly $100 an hour apiece; and a public relations wizard from Washington, D.C., Pat Korten, was employed at an estimated $250 an hour.

John Douglas interviewed the Ramseys and—surprise!—

announced that they did not fit the profile of child killers. The handwriting experts similarly concluded that neither Ramsey parent had written the ransom note (a number of objective experts would later study the note in depth and decide that while they couldn't make a definitive statement about the authorship, the handwriting most closely resembled Patsy Ramsey's).

After speaking once more with Hunter, I called Ellis Armistead, a former Denver cop who was now the Ramseys' lead private investigator. He had become largely invisible; he gave no interviews and little indication of his actions. His role intrigued me.

We made an appointment for the following afternoon at my home. When he arrived, he rattled my visual expectations. He was crowding seven feet tall and wore a pin-striped suit with a modestly hip red tie. He did not merely walk; he lumbered. He had a big, open face, a stilted blond haircut, a rural manner, and huge hands. His voice was slow and southern-flavored—he had graduated from Vanderbilt University in Nashville—and he reeked of politeness and sincerity. I could see why the Ramseys had hired him.

I hung up his coat and we went down to my basement workroom, where we played information poker for a while. I was not quite sure what I wanted to say to him and it was quickly apparent that he, in the best tradition of private investigators everywhere, did not want to give up anything. As he talked about his background in law enforcement, I kept wondering whether he was really searching for JonBenet's killer or just giving the team a more solid image. Would the family really pay him around $100 an hour not to find out what had happened? And if so, then what was he doing for his money?

Armistead assured me that the Ramseys were committed to pursuing all reasonable leads and that his only job was to find out who had murdered their daughter. He was interested, he emphasized, in any useful information. As he spoke, he exuded seriousness, integrity, and doggedness. He may have been tight-lipped, but he was not oily or mean-spirited. When given the chance, he refused to criticize the Boulder Police Department or the D.A.'s office for their handling of the case. This was a very difficult and delicate situation for everyone, he said, because of the enormous media coverage.

After thirty minutes of chatter, he dropped a sliver of his politeness and asked why I had called him.

"This crime," I said, "could be about something larger than the death of one little girl."

He did not respond and his long, friendly face revealed nothing.

"And perhaps," I went on, "more people were involved than just one or two."

His eyes widened a notch, as if this were not quite what he had been expecting. He stared at me and although we had never seen each other before this afternoon, the feeling in the room was strangely intimate. Some common, if bumpy, ground lay between us. I was an amateur investigator who had spent many years writing books about murders. He was a former cop and a professional gumshoe. His reputation suggested that he was a very good investigator with a strong moral compass. I sensed that he really did want to know the truth behind JonBenet's death, but was not entirely comfortable with the circumstances in which he now found himself. Whether or not he was compromised by working for the Ramseys, he was not entirely free in his duties.

The air inside my workroom was filled with complex feelings and possibilities.

"What do you mean by more than one or two people being involved?" he asked.

I hesitated and then said, "Have you looked into child pornography?"

His expression became more intensely focused.

"That's crossed my mind," he said with a soft twang.

"Have you looked at things on the Internet?"

He just barely shook his head.

"Are you interested in these areas?"

"I'm interested in anything that's significant. Do you know something about this?"

I stared at him, uncertain what to say. He may have already been exploring the realm of child pornography himself, but it was just as likely that he knew nothing about this subject and did not want to reveal his ignorance to me. It was possible that he would use any information he could gather from me or any other source to help create the impression of a murder scenario that pointed toward the Ramseys' innocence.

"I've been taking a look into these things," I said, but offered nothing more.

"Have you found anything?"

"I'm still poking around."

He nodded, but remained silent.

I asked if he had investigated child beauty pageants.

"Not yet," he said.

"Are you going to?"

"I think so."

The room became still. It was soon apparent that the discussion would not go much further, on either side. Armistead thanked me for meeting with him and rose from his chair. I accompanied him upstairs, where we shook hands and he said goodbye and walked out to his car. As I started back down to the basement, the doorbell rang. It was Armistead. He apologized and said he had forgotten his coat, so I retrieved it from the hall closet and we parted once again.

On a couple of occasions later that afternoon, I remembered the coat incident, which may not have meant much, but it did tell me two things. Armistead had been listening, and he had been thinking.

7

By the mid-nineties, taking questionable or risqué pictures of youngsters was not the only activity surrounding the child beauty pageant world that had been normalized. Six-year-old girls were also dying their hair to make it blonder; changing the color of their eyes to make them bluer; capping their teeth or slipping in new ones to make their smiles more ideal; having plastic surgery to "fix" their faces; and cinching up their chests with tape to make it appear that they had cleavage. An entire industry had grown up around child pageants, represented by magazines like *Babette's Talent* and *Pageant Gazette,* which had chosen JonBenet for its cover before her murder and featured her as the cover model after she was killed.

Mothers (mostly) now spent vast amounts of time and money training and dressing their small daughters in exotic costumes so they could win more trophies or dollars at pageant competitions. In the wake of the Ramsey homicide, it became commonplace to hear that child pageants were mostly found in the American south, but in reality, these events were now a nationwide phenomenon, reaching from coast to coast and from Dixie up to the Canadian border. The press had somehow overlooked a multibillion-dollar industry that by December 1996 was flourishing everywhere.

Each year, 250,000 young girls took the stage to pursue this kind of glory. Their parents paid $25 to $500 for entry fees, $200 to $500 for professional photo shoots, and hundreds or thousands more for modeling coaches, dance instructors, voice instructors, and smile instructors. Some girls wore $50 outfits and some donned $2,000 gowns. Roughly 3,000 pageant systems operated in hotel ballrooms or malls across the nation.

Anyone could open a pageant franchise, charge an entry fee, lure in contestants, and put on a show. Anyone could judge the competition. Fraud in the industry had caused Ted Cohen, the president of the Miami-based International Directory of Pageants, to lobby Congress to pass a national licensing law establishing consistent standards and regulations.

The girls began by competing in hometown or regional meets, then advanced to state or national finals. With each step up, the entry fees increased, as did the prizes. A child could earn $10,000 for a weekend win.

Suzi Doland ran the America's Royale Miss pageant in Denver (at her death, JonBenet was the America's Royale Miss reigning queen).

"We've recently had an influx of people, and their kinds of pageants, from the south," Doland said after the murder. "Southern pageants are very different from ours. It's difficult to express that difference without getting negative. We have more of a focus on talent than on the appearance of the child. We have rules governing make-up and things like that. I don't condone what they do in the south, and their influence has been leaking over into this part of the country.

"One good thing that can come out of JonBenet's death is for us to learn that pageants are for kids and overglamourizing them is not necessary or okay. Patsy Ramsey was from the south and she got a lot of advice on how to dress JonBenet and how to model her, and I think a lot of it was bad advice."

With twenty-three years of experience in the field, Eleanor Von Duyke, Denver's best-known pageant organizer and the owner of Show Biz USA, claimed that the publicity following JonBenet's murder did not hurt her business, but caused it to double.

"I haven't seen any bad side effects since the child's death," she said in April 1997. "The pageants are booming, bigger than ever. What people don't understand is that this could have happened to anyone in ice skating or baseball or anywhere else. JonBenet was a normal little kid who dressed in blue jeans and T-shirts. But when she competed around here, she stuck out like a sore thumb because she had that classic southern look: bleached blonde hair and blue eyes and thousand-dollar dresses."

Von Duyke, while a fervent supporter of child pageants, did not view them naively. "Pageants are a cutthroat business. Some directors out there cut other beauty pageants' throats because they want the business for themselves. And some stage mothers can be bad. A lot of kids are only doing this because their mothers want them to and they want to please them. A few years ago, one of our contestants began breaking trophies and chairs because she didn't win. We have the yucky stuff, but people really don't know about it."

"We have a lot of very good and loving mothers in the pageant world," Pam Griffin, a local seamstress who had made JonBenet's pageant dresses, has said. "But we also have some mean ones, who start yelling at their girls the moment they walk off the stage. It's a mixture of the two."

Some mothers have withdrawn their girls from competitions because of "yucky stuff" that went beyond breaking trophies and chairs. I heard anecdotes about men who had been banned from attending child pageants because of their predilection for child molestation; about pageant judges who traded prizes for certain kids in exchange for sex from their mothers; about what occasionally happened with small girls when their mothers were not around.

Entering the pageant world could be, for some girls, like venturing farther and farther into the forest of the adult world. Most of the time, they were protected from the desires and impulses of that world, but sometimes they went there without a protector and did not necessarily report back to a mother or father everything that went on. Why should they? They were only doing what their parents had encouraged them to do.

"My seven-year-old daughter," one mother told me, "really enjoyed the pageants because to her they were like playacting, and that was fun. But she was learning how to draw attention to herself from judges and other adults who were more or less strangers. She liked doing that, because the feedback was great: 'You're so pretty and talented!' This made her feel very grown-up and kids love that feeling. She was learning how to put on a facade that could have been interpreted by some people as a sexual facade. To her it was just an act, but it could stimulate some adults in inappropriate ways—and that frightened me."

8

One April evening, Jeff Shapiro, the young *Globe* freelancer, phoned me.

"Dude," he said, "I am so pissed."

"Why's that?"

"The Ramseys have been moving around town from one house to another. They're trying to hide from us, but they can't. We keep tracking them down and listening to their conversations. We're like the old KGB in the Soviet Union. Yesterday, my boss told me to search through the garbage behind the home they were staying in. So I did and you know what?"

"What?"

"It was the wrong fuckin' house! I went through all their trash in the middle of the night and I wasn't even at the right place. Do you know what that's like?"

"Sounds rough."

"It really sucked, bro."

The more I listened to Shapiro, the more I felt that he was coming to represent the prevailing spirit of the Ramsey case: widespread chaos.

"Look, dude," he said, "you gotta help me out. I'm pumped for this chick but her mother's standing in my way. She doesn't want her daughter to go out with me."

"Huh," I replied.

"Her mother is severely retarded. She thinks the Ramseys are innocent. It's, like, total denial. She can't admit that Patsy went berserk and tortured the kid first—penetrating her with her finger or something else. Then she bashed her over the head and gave her an eight-inch-long concussion. Then she strangled her. I can't let Patsy get away with this. I knew she was psycho the first time I saw her on television."

"You did?"

"Yeah. You can tell a killer by studying the body language. Watch her face. Listen to the way she talks. She isn't smooth, but jerky and guilty."

"If you lose a child, it's pretty hard to be smooth."

"Especially if you garotted her to death. I've got a plan and I need your assistance."

"My assistance?" I said cautiously.

"I have to show this chick's mother that I agree with her about the murder, even though she's wrong. If she thinks that I think the way she thinks about the Ramseys, she'll let me go out with her daughter."

"Okay."

"I wrote up a couple of pages showing how a secret Iranian police force came to Boulder on Christmas night and killed JonBenet because they were angry at John Ramsey because he runs Access Graphics, which is a company that's owned by Lockheed Martin, which is part of the United States military establishment. Muslim fundamentalists believe in death for anyone aligned with the evil American war machine. My document shows how they snuffed out Jon-Benet to get back at her father. I gave these pages to the girl's mom and she was blown away. She thinks I'm a genius."

"She does?"

"Yeah. She faxed my pages off to Geraldo Rivera's people and a couple of his staff members just called me to see if I wanted to go on his show and talk about this Iranian police force. They thought my theory was awesome."

That didn't surprise me. Until 1994, Rivera had been viewed merely as a self-indulgent TV personality, but once the O.J. Simpson case began, he suddenly became an expert on the legal system. Long before the evidence was presented at that trial, he had decided that the defendant was guilty and broadcast that opinion thousands of times throughout O.J.'s sixteen months in prison, his subsequent acquittal, and on into the future; Rivera's personal feelings were far more important than due process. Then he "tried" the Ramsey parents on television—*again without knowing the evidence*—and found them guilty, of course. But in 1998, a curious thing happened to Rivera. After many people started publicly accusing President Clinton of committing high crimes and impeachable offenses, Rivera, who had his own history of infidelity, cried foul and tried to defend the Chief Executive against his attackers. His audience wasn't in a listening mood.

"I told Geraldo's people," Shapiro said, "that I was real busy and can't go on their program. I'm not really busy, but I can't say any of this stuff about the Iranian police on the air."

"Why not?"

"The editors I work for would kill me. They know Patsy's guilty and John helped cover up the crime and they don't want us saying or writing anything else. So I told Geraldo's people to call you and I gave them your number."

"Why me?"

"Because I thought you could help me with this. If they call and invite you on the show, maybe you can tell Geraldo how credible I am."

I couldn't think of a response.

"My credibility is growing every day," he said. "The D.A.'s office talks to me now and I've been talking a lot more to the cops. I think they're both using me to communicate back and forth to each other, because they're having problems working together. The fact is, they hate each other."

"You told the Geraldo show to call me?"

"Yeah. They want you to confirm my Iranian theory. Can you tell them you think it's pretty cool?"

"Well . . ."

"Thanks, bro. I gotta run."

Twenty minutes later, two of Rivera's minions phoned and asked if I could back up Shapiro's story. They wanted me to appear on the air to talk about his ideas, but I passed. The young journalist was disappointed in me and the girl's mother refused to budge.

9

For months after JonBenet's murder, Hal Haddon and his associates jockeyed with the D.A. and the Boulder police over the proper time, location, and rules for a police interrogation of the Ramseys. In late April, a date and place were finally settled upon, but things quickly fell apart. In the next twenty-four hours, Haddon wrote a scorching letter to Hunter, which was released to the media and appeared the next day, in its entirety, in the local papers. It was obviously intended to embarrass the D.A. and show what awaited him in the court-room if he dared bring murder charges against the dead girl's parents. It read:

> Dear Mr. Hunter, by this letter we express our profound dismay at yesterday's actions by the leader-ship of the Boulder Police Department. After repre-sentatives of the Boulder Police Department and your office requested and agreed to a format for separate interviews of John and Patsy Ramsey beginning at 9:30 A.M. today, we were advised at approximately 4:00 P.M. yesterday afternoon that the interviews were canceled because Boulder Police Department leadership no longer agreed to the format of the inter-views—despite previous statements to the contrary.
> When we received this information from your

office yesterday, we offered to discuss any additional matters which might facilitate the interviews, but no one from the Police Department was willing to even have that discussion. In view of the bizarre position of the Police Department, we then offered to make Mr. and Mrs. Ramsey available this morning for separate interviews by Detective Lou Smit and any member of the district attorney's office who wished to attend. This offer was also declined.

This action is incomprehensible in light of the previous history of this case. The Police Department, directly and through a campaign of leaks and smears, has portrayed the Ramseys as unwilling to grant police interviews or assist the investigation. Although we know this innuendo to be false, we have avoided criticizing the police because we believed that it would only fuel a media war which would be counterproductive to the overarching goal—finding and prosecuting the killer of JonBenet Ramsey. Yesterday's actions make further silence untenable. ...

On Friday, April 11, 1997, John and Patsy Ramsey, with their attorneys, met with Peter Hofstrom of your office and Tom Wickman of the Boulder Police Department. This meeting was held at Mr. Hofstrom's request. The Ramseys were told at that meeting that they had been treated unfairly in the past and that authorities wanted to put the investigation on a new track. They were told that "we need your help to solve this crime." The Ramseys were asked to give interviews and continue their previous cooperation. No conditions were placed on the manner in which the interviews would be conducted and, in fact, we were invited to propose any conditions we considered reasonable. At that meeting, John Ramsey immediately said that he would gladly meet with your representatives if it would help the effort to find his daughter's killer.

The day after that meeting, Patsy Ramsey voluntarily provided a fourth handwriting sample [all these samples were used to see if they matched the handwriting in the ransom note]. The Ramseys also agreed to let the authorities search their house again without a warrant; agreed to destructive testing of materials located at their home; agreed to identify Patsy Ramsey's prior writings; and agreed to make themselves available for separate interviews on Wednesday, April 23, 1997, beginning at 9:30 A.M. The Ramseys agreed to answer any questions put to them by any investigator chosen by your office or the Police Department. We requested that these interviews be of two-hour durations, respectively, but we were certainly flexible on time and your agencies voiced no objection to that time frame.

All the arrangements for these interviews had been made and agreed upon. John and Patsy were anxious to participate, based on Mr. Hofstrom's representations that such interviews would assist in apprehending the killer of their daughter. We cannot describe their anguish and disappointment when we were forced to advise them that the police had reneged on the very interviews you earnestly requested on April 11. . . .

This episode is the latest in an inexplicable series of events which appear to be senseless efforts to intimidate and smear the Ramseys without any valid investigative purpose. We can document that both John and Patsy Ramsey were extensively interviewed by Boulder police, including detectives, on Dec. 26, 1996, the day that JonBenet's body was discovered. John Ramsey answered more police questions the next day. On doctors' directions, Patsy Ramsey was not interrogated on Dec. 27.

What occurred next was the most insensitive action in this case, at least to date. Boulder police refused to release JonBenet's body for burial unless the Ramseys agreed to come to the police station and submit to a hostile interrogation. We had to threaten legal action to obtain her release for burial. This was the first in a series of insensitive and incomprehensible actions by the Boulder Police Department leadership to destroy every sincere attempt to have an open and honest relationship with the Boulder Police Department.

After John and Patsy returned from the funeral, we offered to make them available for a joint interview on Jan. 18, 1997, at 10:00 A.M. We told the police that Patsy was too ill to attend the entire session but that John Ramsey would answer all the questions put to him. The police declined this offer and stated in writing that such an interview would not "be helpful" because "the time for interviewing John and Patsy as witnesses who could provide crucial information that would be helpful in the initial stages of our investigation has passed." The police countered with an offer that the Ramseys come to the police station at 6:00 P.M. on a Friday night and subject themselves to inquisition for as long as "the nature and quality of the information" warranted.

That absurd suggestion was rejected, especially since the police did not believe that the Ramseys possessed any "critical information."

Since that time, law enforcement authorities from several agencies have launched a cowardly smear campaign against John and Patsy, fueled by leaks and smears attributable only to "sources." We will no longer endure these tactics in silence. It is beyond comprehension that law enforcement authorities prefer to leak information rather than interrogate the persons who they characterize as "suspects" in the investigation.

It is apparent that the leadership in the Boulder Police Department lacks the objectivity and judgment necessary to find the killer of JonBenet Ramsey. Mr. Hofstrom told John and Patsy that he wanted their help to solve this crime. They remain willing to meet with Mr. Smit, Mr. Ainsworth or any other members of your office to that end.

On April 30, one week after this letter appeared in the papers, the police interviewed the Ramseys separately. No leaks emerged from these talks, but the following day, the Ramseys held their first press conference since January 1. The events leading up to it, apparently managed by Hal Haddon and his associates, conjured up a well-worn script from a TV melodrama.

On the night before the conference, Haddon left a furtive voice-mail message with seven carefully selected local reporters. He told them to be in Boulder with a photographer or cameraman at 10:00 A.M., asked for their pager numbers, and said they would be contacted soon with further instructions. At a little before 10:00 the next morning, they were paged, given a secret password (Subtract), told where to come for the press conference, and sworn to secrecy about the location.

They were also given strict guidelines for dealing with John and Patsy Ramsey: They could take no exterior shots of the building they were coming to; ask no questions about facts relating to the murder or about the parents' recent police interrogation; have no interaction with, or take pictures of, the Ramseys' attorneys, who were also present; and take no photographs of the Ramseys as they arrived or left the premises. This was to be a live, nationally televised event, in which the parents were given free air time so that Americans everywhere would have another opportunity to look at, listen to, and perhaps sympathize with them. The two things Haddon obviously feared the most were journalistic boldness and spontaneity, but he needn't have worried about either one.

The reporters did precisely as they were told. They sat in front of the couple, stared at them as if they were extraterrestrials, and posed a series of harmless questions. When someone asked the Ramseys why they had picked these seven scribes, Patsy said, "You were all kind of leading journalists in your field, and there are a lot of wacky journalists that have been following us around and they don't have a real picture of us."

John Ramsey looked both calm and stunned. Patsy appeared as she had last January 1: volatile, emotional, angry, and on the edge of tears. From the start, they were on the offensive:

"To those of you who may want to ask," John Ramsey said, "let me address very directly: I did not kill my daughter, JonBenet. There have also been innuendoes that she has been or was sexually molested. I can tell you those were the most hurtful innuendoes to us as a family. They are totally false. JonBenet and I had a very close relationship. I will miss her dearly for the rest of my life."

"I'm Patsy Ramsey," his wife said, "JonBenet's mother, and I'm grateful that we are finally able to sit together face to face. I'm appalled that anyone would think that either John or I could be involved in such a hideous, heinous crime. But let me assure you that I did not kill JonBenet. I did not have anything to do with it. I loved that child with [the] whole of my heart and soul.

"We made a firm commitment that we would not speak openly until we had spent time with the authorities. That was successfully accomplished yesterday, and now we we feel like it's time to talk with all of you. Quite frankly, over the past months, it has not been easy to talk with anyone. As with anyone who has suffered the loss of a child, this is a time spent with family and friends and clergy people and, quite frankly, a lot of time in prayer. We feel like God has a master plan for all of us and that in the fullness of time our family will be united again, and we will see JonBenet.

"We need to all work together as a team, and we need your help. Some of you may have seen the ad that we placed in our local *Daily Camera* newspaper this past weekend. This reward money [now $100,000, double the earlier amount] has been offered since the death of JonBenet, but we felt like it wasn't getting out to the public enough. So this ad with her most recent kindergarten picture will be appearing more and more frequently. And what we want to let everyone know is that this $100,000 is for information leading to the arrest and conviction of the killer of our daughter."

Patsy bristled at the suggestion that placing her young child in beauty pageants might have had a negative effect on

JonBenet, and then she said something strange and provocative, something that seemed completely unrehearsed:

"We feel that there are at least two people on the face of this earth who know who did this, and that is the killer and someone that person may have confided in."

Her husband swung his head in her direction and gazed at his wife, but did not speak.

"Please, please," Patsy said, "if you know anything, I beg you to call us."

"We have," John said, "supplied them [the Boulder police] with every piece of information we have. And frankly ... we were ... insulted that we would even be considered suspects in the death of our daughter, and felt that an interrogation of us was a waste of our time and a waste of the police's time, but because we have to do this, we had to do it."

Then he also did something unpredictable and addressed the killer: "We'll find you. We will find you. I have that as the sole mission for the rest of my life."

"Likewise ..." Patsy said, pointing straight into the camera, clenching her teeth and conveying a maternal fierceness. "You may be eluding the authorities for a time, but God knows who you are and we will find you.... We would like to think that we don't know anyone that we've ever met in our lives that would ever do such a thing to a child ... but they [the police] talked with us and said, 'Please, tell us the names of people you know who may have been in your home at any time.' We just outpoured information, as much as we could try to remember...."

"We think," John Ramsey said, "we are a normal American family that loves and values their children, much like most of the families in this country."

"We have so many emotions...." Patsy said. "I talk to

JonBenet and I tell her I love her and I will be seeing her real soon and it won't be long."

Following the press conference, pundits devoted many hours to analyzing the couple's body language, their interaction on camera, their words and speech patterns. A few even played Patsy's sentences backwards in their search for clues that she had killed her little girl. People ripped her for calling JonBenet "my child," instead of something more intimate and warmer. Others vilified John for being distant or cold to his wife onscreen. And many observers said that Patsy's surprising remark about "two people on the face of this earth" knowing who committed the murder was an obvious reference to her husband and herself. Wasn't that why John had suddenly looked at her? Hadn't she just confessed to the whole world?

I came away from the press conference with one overriding impression. It is extremely rare, even in this time of massive public relations campaigns, for an attorney to allow his or her clients, when they are standing in the midst of serious legal trouble, to appear before the media and speak on the record. This recommendation of silence often holds true for those who have already been acquitted in trials, as well as for those who have been found guilty. While convicted felons, including those who have received lifetime sentences, may appear to have nothing to lose by talking, smart lawyers are notorious for telling them to keep quiet and to stay away from reporters. The less said on the record, the better.

It is also rare for a good attorney to allow his or her clients to appear on television and lie outright. It simply exposes them to too many potential problems later on. To take the cynical view for the moment, lying in public is what some people pay their lawyers to do for them.

Hal Haddon, according to those who admired him and those who did not, was a good, smart lawyer. Given that, and given his obvious desire to shape the Ramseys' media image, I could not help but wonder if he were playing the old eye-of-the-needle legal game. Had the Ramseys been coached to tell the facts within a very narrow range of the truth, and leave out everything else? Had they slimmed down their version of events to fit neatly inside a small opening, while ignoring what was not so neat or containable? If this were the case, then they could, indeed, orchestrate a press conference, appear on national television, and accomplish two things at once: not tell everything they knew, but not lie, either. That strategy fit perfectly with the two-sided nature of so many aspects of the homicide.

From the very beginning, the case had been framed, by the media and perhaps by the legal system itself, as an either-or murder. Either the Ramseys had killed their daughter and covered it up, or an intruder had broken into their home on Christmas night and committed the crime. I had never heard anybody discuss, at least on the public airwaves, any other options.

What had repeatedly struck me, once one hundred days had passed without an arrest in the case, was that neither scenario was necessarily true. Weren't there any number of possibilities that lay in between these two? What if there were something more behind the face of the murder, something complicated and obscure, in which the parents were involved without actually participating in the murder? Why were we limited to a single pair of thoughts about the homicide?

What if everyone—from Peter Boyles, who insisted the Ramseys were guilty, to Hal Haddon, who insisted they were innocent—was right about the case? What if the Ramseys were guilty and innocent at the same time? What if *who* had killed her was ultimately less significant than *what* had killed her? And what if the bitterly adversarial arguments over the murder had illuminated nothing?

Why could we safely assume that both parents knew exactly what had occurred that Christmas night? Why would John Ramsey have hired a set of attorneys for himself and another for his wife, unless he had perceived at least a potential conflict of interest between himself and Patsy? But where was the conflict in the case (it hadn't publicly emerged yet) or the crack in the facade? If Patsy's maternal anger and ferocity were as genuine as they appeared to be, would she have been able to protect her husband from a murder charge? And most intriguing of all: If one parent were guilty, was the other being used for subtle purposes? How did the bonds of marriage and the depths of parenthood and the secrets that reside inside every human heart figure into all of this?

As simple as many people wanted the homicide's scenario to be, the behavior of John and Patsy Ramsey suggested otherwise.

In the days following the press conference, a poster offering $100,000 for information about the murder of JonBenet Ramsey began appearing around Boulder. Inevitably, somebody replaced the girl's picture with her father's and changed the message to read that the reward was for the arrest and conviction of the murderer—John Ramsey himself. The new flyer was quickly plastered all over town.

10

In early May, I returned to the Boulder County Jail for another visit with the inmate I had questioned earlier. This time he gave me the names of several people who he claimed were involved in adult or child pornography. Through other sources, I was able to confirm that at least two of these individuals were, in fact, in the possession of extensive child pornography libraries. One of them, a lawyer, had left Boulder a few months prior to the murder. I tracked him down in another state. He denied that he had ever been connected to child pornography, but acknowledged that he knew local people who were. Another Boulder attorney admitted that he had clients who were engaged in child porn, but that he was ethically bound not to reveal their identities. A third person had once had an interest in taking risqué photographs of teenagers, but had long since given up this pursuit.

One name in particular, however, was of more interest to me. Political activists in Boulder had previously identified him as a city employee who had had connections to pornography and perhaps child pornography. According to these sources, a number of years earlier, two municipal workers had found illicit sexual material and erotic toys in this man's desk. Although female coworkers had previously alleged sexual harassment, none of them had initiated any legal action against him. Eventually, they were assigned to another office. According to city council members, Boulder's mayor, Leslie Durgin, had at first wanted to fire the man, but after consulting with others, had decided not to. The incident was never made public, and the local newspaper, the *Daily Camera,* while aware of these events, did not carry the story because no one was willing to speak on the record. It was a scandal that never erupted.

Following my second meeting with the inmate, I returned to Alex Hunter's office at the Boulder County Justice Center. After passing along some information about Internet pornography and the names of local people I had been investigating, I brought up the story about the city employee. Hunter appeared taken aback by this, almost alarmed, and he expressed concern that something like this had gone on inside the municipal government. He seemed amazed that anything of this nature could have happened without his knowledge. Twice he asked me if I was talking about the same man whom he had known for many years, although he had not had much interaction with him. Twice I assured him that I was.

"If this got into the hands of certain people in the media," Hunter said, "it would further embarrass Boulder and make the town look worse than it already does. What are you going to do with this information?"

I explained that I was not really concerned with the man's sexual behavior and had no desire to publicize it unless it was somehow connected to the Ramsey case. What I was concerned with was whether Hunter's office planned to investigate the pornography leads we recently had been discussing.

"I'm personally very interested in this angle," he said, "but we have other priorities. It's on the list of things to do, but it's not even close to the top."

It had been very difficult, he said, to get the police to explore leads they did not want to explore, especially those that did not specifically concern the Ramsey family. Moreover, from the start of the case, his relationship with the Boulder Police Department had been shaky. Hunter surprised me by stating that John Eller, the commander in charge of the detectives investigating the murder, was "impossible to work with" in these circumstances. Eller, the D.A. declared, had long focused on only one thing: arresting John and Patsy Ramsey.

"The cops," Hunter said, "regard us as intruders in this situation. That makes everything tougher. I don't have enough to file a case against the Ramseys. The cops keep bringing me things and saying, 'How much is enough, how much is enough?' We're not there yet."

"Do you think you'll get there soon?"

"I just don't know," he said with a deep frown.

The more I talked to Hunter, the more I saw him as the man in the middle of a huge, multifaceted vise. From one side, the police felt he was not doing his job because he was not ready to bring charges against the Ramseys—and the cops were leaking these sentiments to reporters. From another side, Hal Haddon and his legal juggernaut had absolutely no qualms about publicly flailing Hunter whenever they felt it served their purposes. From yet another side, Hunter was attacked daily on radio and TV shows for his perceived ineptitude (the press kept digging up cases unsuccessfully prosecuted by the D.A.'s office, starting with the murder of Sid Wells, the boyfriend of Robert Redford's daughter, back in 1983). Finally, the general population, through its participation on these talk shows, also viewed Hunter as a weak, ineffectual authority figure who could not get the job done, a job many of them felt was easy to carry out. As time went on, the vise from all sides tightened further around Hunter.

Although Hunter did not complain about his situation to

me, I sensed that it was having a very real effect on him. He looked subdued, weighed down. His eyes were furtive, his voice had grown softer. It was almost as if, without even being aware of it, he had spent many years readying himself, or failing to ready himself, for a test that he could never quite have imagined would come. Now it had arrived and he had to muddle his way through it while suffering chastisements from every corner. He had to trust his own instincts and listen to himself rather than the ten thousand other loud voices that knew less than he did but were telling him what to do.

After I gave him the information I had obtained about child pornography and the Internet, Hunter leaned back in his chair and spread a legal pad across his lap, speculating about who had killed JonBenet Ramsey. Once again I was struck by the informality of his behavior and his willingness to share his ideas. He thought some of John Andrew Ramsey's fraternity brothers at the Chi Psi house at the University of Colorado may have gotten high Christmas night and, during an aborted attempt to kidnap JonBenet and make some easy money, accidentally killed her and then concocted the note as a cover-up.

After laying out this scenario, Hunter looked directly at me, awaiting my response.

For several moments, I said nothing. I was thinking about this unexpected angle. First of all, it didn't square with any of the current theories about the crime, including one of the very few solid facts in the case: that John Andrew Ramsey had been in Atlanta the night the girl was killed. Second, I had assumed that in the first month after the murder, both the Boulder cops and the scores of reporters covering the case had fully questioned the frat brothers; to my knowledge, no one had learned anything of substance from them. Third, if Hunter's scenario were accurate, some lesser participant might eventually have talked to and made a deal with the authorities in exchange for immunity from prosecution; that had not happened. Fourth, and most important, Hunter had not delivered this possibility to me with what I took to be real conviction. It almost seemed as if this were what the D.A. *wished* had happened to JonBenet.

I wondered if something more was going on in the room, but what could that be?

"The frat boys might have been involved," I said without much enthusiasm. Hunter did not press the matter.

I then asked him if he had ever spoken to Pam Griffin, the local seamstress who, through her work on JonBenet's pageant dresses, had gotten to know Patsy and her daughter quite well. Hunter said he had not talked to her but indicated that it was also on his list of things to do.

"I think you should call her," I said.

11

Middle-aged and attractive, Pam Griffin reminded me of a country-and-western singer who had seen both ends of the barrel but was finally on top and enjoying life. Everything about her conjured up gumption and grit. She was dark-haired, hawk-eyed, outspoken, and she naturally put into words what she felt and perceived. Talk flowed from her. She was also an ex-nurse with a degree in pediatric psychiatry. She had seen a great deal of human life and had extremely strong feelings about protecting youngsters.

On the afternoon of December 26, 1996, Griffin and her teenage daughter, Kristine, had gone shopping. They returned to their suburban Boulder home at 7:00 P.M. When Griffin listened to her phone messages, she heard a faint female voice sounding vaguely like Patsy Ramsey's asking her to come over and mentioning something about a child. She heard another similar, hushed message from Priscilla, Fleet White's wife (Pam later told me that this call had been made from inside a closet). Griffin, busy with some holiday house guests and unsure that she understood either message, decided to return the calls the next morning. At 10:00 P.M. that night, she flipped on the TV news, paying little attention until a story came on about a local six-year-old girl who had been found dead earlier in the day.

"I saw JonnyB's picture on the screen," Griffin said in early April 1997, "and it was just a total shock. I tried to call Patsy right away, but I couldn't reach her. Kristine and I jumped in the car and drove down to the Ramsey house. We got there in about ten minutes. Normally, it takes a little longer."

The Ramseys' residence was decorated for the Christmas season. A jolly plastic Santa Claus near a lamp was covered with ivy. Two-feet-tall red-and-white candy canes lined the sidewalk leading up to the front door. Now another color was added: Yellow police tape surrounded the home, keeping gawkers off the lawn.

"I parked near the house," Griffin says. "Kristine and I got out and tried to walk closer, but the police told us to get back in the car. They asked us how we knew the Ramseys."

During that year, Pam had sewn pageant dresses for Jon-Benet. Kristine—who by age three had herself been a success on the pageant circuit and who was now being groomed for an acting career—was the girl's modeling coach, teaching her the stage moves she needed to win the pageants.

After giving this information to the police, both women began to cry. For an hour, they sat in front of the Ramseys' home, watching cops, medics, and other officials move in and out of the house. Around midnight, the medics brought Jon-Benet's small body outside and slipped it into the rear of a vehicle.

"That was not something I would have wanted Kristine to see," Griffin told me, "but it was too late for that."

The Griffins rode home and went to bed. Early the next morning, on December 27, Patsy's sister, Pamela, phoned and asked Griffin to come visit them at the home of John and Barbara Fernie, friends of the Ramseys. The seamstress arrived at 9:00 A.M. and stayed until late afternoon. Female friends of the Ramseys had gathered at the house cooking and talking, while the men wandered from room to room and spoke among themselves.

"John Ramsey looked absolutely gray that day," Griffin remembers. "Just completely shaken."

Patsy looked worse. As a former nurse, Griffin knew at once that Patsy had been heavily sedated (she was receiving a dose of Valium every three hours). Fearing that Patsy was becoming toxic, Griffin insisted that she drink a lot of liquids. "We kept giving her water and she joked that we were trying to drown her," she told me. "When she needed to go to the bathroom, I took her there and stood by the door. She came out and lay down on the bed, really groggy. I sat beside her, waiting for her to fall asleep. She reached up and touched the side of my face. She just rambled and rambled. 'Fix this, Pam,' she said, almost begging me. 'Fix this, please.' I said, 'I can't, honey. I can't fix it.' She said, 'I bring you things that aren't beautiful and you make them beautiful. You always make things better. Make this go away.' I told her I couldn't do that and she drifted off to sleep. It was a desperate plea."

In her medical work, Griffin had seen many people in drugged states of desperation and had heard numerous bedside confessions. "I truly believe that if Patsy had been hiding something, she would have told me right then, before she fell asleep. That's when people say things, whether they mean to or not. But she didn't tell me anything that indicated she knew something about JonBenet's death. If she had, I'll tell you right now—I would not have protected her."

Later that day, near dusk, Griffin spoke to Sergeant Larry Mason of the Boulder Police Department, one of the officers who had come to the Ramseys' home the day before. He asked her about the kinds of discipline the Ramseys used with their children: Had she ever seen John or Patsy lose control with JonBenet or her brother, Burke?

No, she told Mason, she had never witnessed any screaming or hitting inside that household; just the opposite. She continually had been impressed by all the affection and hugging that went on between the family members.

"John Ramsey couldn't even spank that little girl," she told me. "When one of his kids got injured, he could hardly function, it hurt him so much. One time at a pageant, I overheard JonBenet talking to her father about her new dress. He said, 'It's important that it's so pretty, honey, but it's more important to develop your talent and the person you are inside, because if anything ever happens to your beauty, you'll still have these other things.' That day JonBenet won the overall talent competition and then went up to her dad and gave him her medal. He's worn it ever since her death.

"Basically, John thought the pageants were stupid, but he went along with them because of Patsy and JonnyB."

Sergeant Mason also asked Griffin if Patsy had been depressed lately because of her struggles with ovarian cancer.

"I told him no again. I told him she was upbeat because she was beating the disease. She looked at cancer as a test and a trial, and she was determined to survive it so she could raise her children. The week before the murder, she said that God had allowed her the time to bring up her kids, but after JonBenet and Burke were grown, she would have a relapse and it would kill her. Her children were everything to her."

Had John Ramsey, the sergeant inquired, ignored his wife during her illness?

"It wasn't like that. Patsy used to tell me, 'I don't see how that man put up with me when I was so sick, but he did.' Back then, her hair was falling out and she threw up every five minutes. John still brought her flowers and intimate things and treated her like a china doll. Last fall, I helped her go to a party as a Southern Belle. We made pantaloons for her and got her a bonnet and she went as Scarlett O'Hara. Later on, she blushed and told me, 'My husband couldn't keep his hands off of me that night.'

"The two of them make a real contrast. John is normally very stoic and businesslike. Patsy is charming and warm. He stands and observes. She mingles and makes people smile. To murder this child, you'd either have to be a monster or not know JonBenet, and her father wasn't either one of those things. You can sense things about men. John Ramsey just didn't have the bloodlust to strangle her and fracture her skull. And Patsy as the killer? Impossible. She's unbelievably good and sweet and generous. If you spent one hour with her, you'd know what I mean.

"During her cancer recovery, she went to an affair at the school to help the children. Her wig got itchy so she tossed it onto the floor. The kids roared at this bald woman standing in front of them, but she told them, 'If it doesn't bother you, it doesn't bother me.' That's just the way she is.

"Patsy had a glow about her, as good people do. It's gone now, cried out of her since JonBenet died. She doesn't look the same. I've always thought that she knew who did this, but she didn't know she knew. She was grieving too much to stop and really think about it. The day after the murder, when she touched my face and asked me to make things better, she kept saying, '*They* took my child, *they* took my child. Of all the children in the world, why did *they* have to do to this to my child?' She didn't say 'I' did it or 'he' did it or 'we' did it. She said, 'Why did *they* come into my house and take one of my children?' It was always *they*. It had to be someone outside of their home."

Griffin had a salty tongue, and she had a lot more to say than had come out during her numerous media appearances since the case had begun. For months, she had appeared on national television—on Geraldo Rivera's daytime program, in particular—acting as something of a spokesperson for the Ramsey family. She was by far their staunchest public defender and had been widely criticized for this. She was not someone easily intimidated or silenced by carping, and until such time as the Ramseys were convicted of a crime, she would commit herself to extending them the presumption of innocence on television. That commitment had deeply annoyed some people inside the pageant world, which was also coming under a lot of criticism in the wake of the homicide, and Griffin's efforts on the Geraldo show would cost her small sewing business many customers and thousands upon thousands of dollars in revenues.

"Patsy Ramsey is worth it to me," she asserts. "She's worth every dime that I've lost."

I once asked Griffin if she remembered anything more than what she had already told me about her visit to Patsy on the day after JonBenet's body was discovered. She said that the most visible and forceful person at the Fernies' home that day was not John Ramsey, but Fleet White, John's best friend before the murder.

"White was everywhere," she told me. "Ordering everyone around. Telling people what to do and not to do. Giving me the creeps. He didn't want me to be alone with Patsy. Didn't want me in the bedroom with her. Didn't want me to help her go to the bathroom. Didn't want me talking to her as she was falling asleep. He didn't even want me to help her drink water to keep her from getting dehydrated. I was trying to assist my friend and couldn't understand why he was acting this way. Someone finally had to tell him to back off, so he took a hike and disappeared."

According to Griffin, White behaved similarly at JonBenet's memorial service at St. John's Episcopal Church the following Sunday, Patsy's fortieth birthday. After the service, the Ramseys and Whites had flown together to Marietta, Georgia, a suburb of Atlanta, for JonBenet's funeral.

"At that time," Griffin said, "White was just very overbearing."

Patsy's mother, the outspoken Nedra Paugh, told the police that in those days White was a "wild man and a lunatic."

After mentioning Pam Griffin to Hunter while we were sitting in his office in early May, I inquired if Fleet White had ever come under any suspicion.

The D.A. studied me inquisitively. "Why do you ask that?"

"Just curious."

The atmosphere in the room had been very relaxed, like a couple of old acquaintances talking away an afternoon over a beer in a tavern, but White's name caused a slight shift in the air.

Hunter said that John Ramsey and White had gotten into a bad argument in Georgia, when they had taken JonBenet there for the burial. The altercation—unreported in the media—had become so heated, the D.A. continued, that the police had to be called in.

"The cops stayed at the house," Hunter said, "for about six hours."

"Six hours?"

"Six hours."

"That's a very long time."

"Yes, it is."

I asked what they were fighting about.

"The Ramseys have never said. White has told us that it

was because he wanted John Ramsey to cooperate more with the authorities and Ramsey said no."

"Why was White so concerned about that?"

"I don't know."

"Do you believe White?"

The D.A. hesitated, and then said, "I've met the man, and he made me very uncomfortable. He's six-foot-four, with big shoulders and huge hands. An iron grip. He just gave me a feeling. We know one thing for sure. The Ramseys and the Whites stopped being friends after the trip to Georgia. That's strange, because they used to go sailing together and had been very close. They'd socialized a lot in the past and the Ramseys had gone over to their home on Christmas night. Both families had young daughters the same age. We've heard that Daphne White was JonBenet's best friend."

"Has anyone talked to Daphne?"

"Social Services has, but I'm not satisfied with what they've done."

"Are you aware," I said, "that Daphne and JonBenet were photographed together?"

"No," he said, jotting something down on a legal pad.

"There was recently a picture of the two of them in the *National Enquirer*. They were all dressed up and it looked like an Easter photo."

"That's very interesting."

White, Hunter said, had given a handwriting sample to the police, but he was ruled out as the author of the ransom note. Because of that, the oil man really was not under any suspicion by the Boulder authorities. Yet, Hunter added, the man's behavior had seemed odd to him.

In recent weeks, the *National Enquirer* had published a cover story headlined COPS FIND MURDER WITNESS. The witness was Fleet White himself, and the article stated that not only had he been with John Ramsey when Ramsey found JonBenet in the wine cellar, but "White has told investigators that Ramsey attempted to keep him from going into the small basement room" where the body had lain. White was "stunned," according to the story, as he watched Ramsey tear duct tape from his child's mouth and destroy other evidence. The Whites and the Ramseys, the *Enquirer* implied, had since had an irrevocable falling out, because Fleet White believed that the Ramseys had killed their little girl.

I asked Hunter about this article and he said, "White had an hysterical reaction when the story came out. He basically begged us to clear his name in connection with the crime. We didn't have any evidence on him, so we did."

"So he's totally cleared?"

"For now he is, but that could change. Why are you concerned about Mr. White? Do you know something more than you're saying?"

I shook my head.

"I just noticed," Hunter said, "that your expression changed when you mentioned him."

I smiled at the D.A. There was something reassuring about the fact that he was this observant.

"According to Pam Griffin," I said, "White was very upset the day after the body was found. Pam told me that he wanted to keep people away from Patsy Ramsey."

"He did?"

"Why would he have been so worried about Patsy?"

"I don't know."

"Why would he have fought so bitterly with John?"

"I don't know."

"What was the real source of the conflict?"

Hunter looked at me and shrugged.

12

That evening, I called Jeff Shapiro, the *Globe* freelancer, and asked if he had spoken with Hunter lately.

"Yeah," he said.

"What about?"

"Santa Claus. They're still looking at him."

Shapiro was referring to Bill McReynolds, a former journalism professor at the University of Colorado, who lived up in the mountains with his wife, Janet; they had been married for thirty-four years. McReynolds had a long white beard, a roundish body, and a cornball poetic way of speaking. He exuded the kind of warmth and fuzziness that charms some people and leave others uncomfortable. For the past three holiday seasons, McReynolds had played Santa Claus at the Ramseys' home. Dressed up like Ol' Saint Nick, he delivered presents to JonBenet and Burke while telling them stories about riding across the sky with his reindeer and big bag of Christmas gifts. He put silver sparkles in his beard and let JonBenet find them, explaining to her that when his reindeer ran into stars, sparkles fell off and landed in his whiskers.

Ever since meeting JonBenet, McReynolds had found her to be a special child. Echoing others, he said that she had a certain "look" and was "luminous." He compared her to an angel. She had, in fact, been a bright, effervescent, and charming girl. She had taken violin and piano lessons and had recently made the Stars Honor Roll at High Peaks Elementary, excelling in math. She liked to sing and dance and to eat macaroni and cheese at home after school while curled up in front of the movies of her favorite star, Shirley Temple. Jon-Benet was somewhat of a natural ham herself, and during the recent High Peaks holiday festivities had dressed up like a Christmas present and sung "Jingle Bell Rock."

At her memorial service, Bill McReynolds had spoken about his relationship with JonBenet, and about some other kids he had known who were no longer alive. He kept a harp at home, he said, and on it he had carved the names of the dead children he had been close to.

Laurie Wagner, a longtime business associate of John Ramsey who worked in public relations at Access Graphics, heard McReynolds speak at the service and was taken aback.

"It was really creepy," she told me, "and others who were there had the same reaction. I think this man really believes that he's Santa Claus. Only an oddball would do that. At the memorial, he described a conversation he'd had with Jon-Benet in her bedroom. It struck me as one of those things you do with children, where the dialogue is so familiar that kids give you a rote response. He asked her where Santa was when he was not with her. 'In my heart,' she said. Then he asked her where she will be when she's gone. 'In Santa's heart,' she told him. These words sent chills up and down my spine. McReynolds told a reporter that he was looking for a place on his harp to put JonBenet's name."

In his role as Santa Claus, McReynolds had hidden gifts in the Ramseys' home. Although he knew the complicated layout of the fifteen-room house—and might have even known his way around it in the middle of the night—he was sixty-seven years old and had had double bypass heart surgery only four months before the murder. He was not supposed to do anything strenuous.

"As I listened to him at the memorial," recalled Wagner, "I could create a scenario that answered all of my questions. He may have had a key to the house and he'd been there as recently as December 23, the night of the party. He may have told JonBenet that he had a present for her down in the basement. It all sort of fit together."

Back in the seventies, Bill McReynolds's nine-year-old daughter had been abducted with a friend of hers in Longmont, Colorado, about an hour away from Boulder. The McReynolds girl was not harmed in the incident, but she did witness the molestation of her friend. Around that same time, Bill's wife, Janet, wrote a play, *Hey, Rube,* which dramatized the sexual assault, torture, and murder of a girl whose body was found in a basement. The play was based upon a 1965 homicide in Indiana. *Hey, Rube* won the 1976 Western States Arts Foundation regional prize and earned Janet McReynolds $7,500 from the National Endowment for the Arts.

When, early in 1997, these details surfaced about Bill and Janet McReynolds, they suddenly became the talk show suspects of the moment; that speculation soon faded away. What was not pursued on the airwaves was that the Ramseys may have been familiar with the play Janet McReynolds had written, just as they were familiar with a book authored by John Douglas, the F.B.I. crime profiler hired by the family following the murder. Douglas's book, *Mind Hunter,* which was retrieved from the Ramseys' home by the police, also contained a section about a child who was abducted and found dead in a basement. Patsy Ramsey, there is reason to believe, was frightened by both of these homicidal scenarios—frightened enough that by late 1996 they were still stirring in her memory.

13

A couple of days after speaking with Alex Hunter about Pam Griffin, I called her at home. She was busy sewing a pageant dress, but she told me that she could talk on the phone and work at the same time. With the machine humming in the background, I asked her about the widespread rumor that Patsy Ramsey had killed her daughter because the child was a chronic bed wetter. Was it possible that JonBenet's mother had finally spun out of control over this intimate and difficult issue, ending the girl's life in a late-night rage?

"JonnyB did have trouble with her bladder," Griffin said. "That's why she made a lot of visits to her pediatrician. About thirty or so from what I've heard in the media. People on the radio keep saying that she went to the doctor because she was being abused down there, but that wasn't the problem. She'd hold urine in her bladder and then it dribbled out. It was an irritant for her. You know kids. They never go to the bathroom when you tell them to.

"This got really bad in the summer of '96. Patsy told her to drink a lot of water because it was good for her skin. JonnyB did this, but then she had to urinate all of it out. Sometimes, she'd be up on stage and have trouble with this and touch herself there. That exasperated Patsy, and she talked about it. But that's all it was—too much water drinking. If Patsy Ramsey ever thought that anyone, including her husband, had laid a hand on her child, she would have destroyed them."

I asked Griffin if she knew any of the local photographers who had taken JonBenet's picture at pageants or elsewhere. "Sure," she said. "A lady in Boulder did some work for Patsy and a man in Palm Springs was advising her about what to put in JonnyB's modeling portfolio. One of her Denver photographers was Mark Fix. The other was Randy Simons."

The first name registered no effect on me, but the second one did. I had read about Simons after the murder and the information had stayed with me. He'd begun his career doing fashion layouts for Denver department stores, but since 1983 had conducted thousands of studio sessions with young girls from all over the Rocky Mountain west. Many people considered him the best, and most expensive, child photographer in the region. He was talented and likeable—a large, big-bellied, friendly man and an incorrigible flirt who liked to hug and flatter his clients as well as their mothers.

In June 1996, Simons had been hired to take "cover girl" pictures of JonBenet at his studio in a Denver suburb. After the child was killed, he had tried to contact the Ramseys to ask what he should do with their daughter's portfolio. The national media was scouring the area for anyone with photos of the victim, ready to pay top prices for her image. The days following the murder were very chaotic for the Ramseys, and Simons could not reach them. He did not know what to do. He was sitting on a treasure trove, but decided to wait until the press discovered his pictures before taking any action.

"I also wanted to make sure I wasn't trying to hide," he somewhat mysteriously told the *Denver Post* in January 1997. "I realized it was going to make me look suspicious if the media wanted these [pictures] so bad and they couldn't find me. People [later] insinuated that I was trying to hide photos of child abuse."

The media soon located Simons on the eastern plains of Colorado and began blitzing him for the right to use the pictures. In the course of several days, he received 248 phone calls regarding his JonBenet portfolio. He became frightened, he told the *Post,* because he was involved in "some weird photographic coup."

In the newspaper article, he portrayed himself as someone who had been faced with the temptation of peddling the pictures for lots of money but who had resisted that option and done the right thing. He had sold his entire JonBenet collection to the Sygma Photo Agency, a national distribution outlet in New York City, for $7,500, plus a percentage of the dollars Sygma received for reselling the photos to newspapers, magazines, and television programs. Sygma now had the pictures, but Simons had kept the negatives in a rural bank vault.

He had let the photos go cheap, he explained to the paper, "because I wanted the pictures to get worldwide coverage so this guy [JonBenet's killer] would have no place to hide."

The *Post* story was fairly routine, except for one thing. It mentioned that Simons had wept during his thirty-minute interview with the reporter, Bill Briggs, and it was this detail, more than any other, that I had retained throughout the past few months.

"What can you tell me about Randy Simons?" I asked Griffin.

"I've known him for fifteen years," she said above the whir of her sewing machine, "and he's photographed my daughter, Kristine, since she was three years old. He loved to tease little girls, but that seemed totally innocent to me. We all loved Randy and were completely comfortable with him.

He had the best pageant photography business around, but for the past year or so, he's lived alone out in eastern Colorado. He left a wife and daughter and son back in Denver. Nobody can figure out why he moved there. He says that he's making or selling antennas for CB radios now. Money was always important to him. He talked about it a lot and was always trying to make more."

"How did he behave after JonBenet's murder?"

"He was very strange and I thought his reactions were inappropriate. He was more torn up than anyone else outside the family, and he'd only met the girl once or twice. He just kept phoning me about JonBenet and crying and crying. He wouldn't stop. When he first called, he wanted me to contact Patsy and get her permission for him to sell JonnyB's portfolio. I couldn't get that permission, so he just went ahead and sold the pictures. Pageant people were really upset with him for doing that. He's been blackballed because of it. We don't want photographers to exploit these children by having their pictures plastered all over the tabloids.

"As time went on after the murder, Randy just became hysterical. It was odd because I'd never heard him cry before about anything. He began calling me late at night and saying that people were going to come out to where he lived and kill him. He had a wild, scary sound in his voice. Then he said something that really stopped me."

"What was that?"

"He said that he didn't have an alibi for the night of last December 25. 'Why do you need an alibi?' I asked him. He wouldn't answer that question. I asked him where he was on Christmas night. He said he didn't want to talk about it. In the past, he'd always wanted to talk about everything. He was extremely upset and it just didn't make any sense to me. If you didn't agree with him now, he got nasty and started screaming like a madman. Maybe he just turned paranoid because people in the beauty pageant world were angry at him and he was losing some business."

In the first weeks of the murder investigation, Pam had been interviewed twice by the Boulder police. Almost all of their questions had focused on the Ramseys' behavior toward their children. They had never asked her about beauty pageants, Randy Simons, or any other photographers.

"The other night," Griffin told me, "Randy called me after midnight. He was sobbing like a child and saying that John and Patsy had done it. In the past, he hadn't said they were guilty, but now he did. I wasn't going along with this and he didn't want to hear me. He was scared out of his mind, and the swings in his mood were really something. This was so unlike him before the death. Don't you think this is weird?"

"You obviously do."

"Why is he so determined to pin it on the Ramseys?"

"I don't know."

The sewing machine had stopped, and Griffin didn't speak for several seconds.

"I put my own daughter in the same circumstances with some of these people that JonBenet was in," she said. "But I never left her alone with photographers. My instincts always told me I shouldn't do that."

"What else do you know, Pam?"

She hesitated, before saying, "One time Randy wanted to shoot Kristine nude, but I said absolutely not. We weren't into that. He had nude pictures laying around his studio, fairly tasteful ones of adult women, so I knew he did this sort of thing, but not with my daughter. Another time he suggested using computer equipment to put Kristine's head on another body, to make her image more salable. They can do anything with computers now and maybe he just wanted to help her career, but I wasn't into that, either."

She drew a long breath, which was followed by another sound that I didn't immediately recognize.

"It makes me wonder what kind of a mother I've been," she said.

I remained silent.

"It makes me wonder what kinds of things I may have exposed my daughter to."

She was crying into the receiver and didn't speak for quite a while. Neither did I.

Then she said, "This is just very painful for me to think about."

Those who were following the Ramsey case—including those affiliated with the media and the legal system—felt that ever since JonBenet's murder, Pam Griffin was little more than a shill for John and Patsy Ramsey. Because of this perception, many observers felt that Pam had no credibility when it came to discussing the case; some even insisted that she would fabricate things in order to cast the Ramseys in a better light. With this in mind, I called several other women on the local pageant scene to ask them about their recent experiences with Randy Simons.

Trish Dampier, Miss Colorado in 1989, ran the "Mrs. Colorado" pageant. Like Pam, she had known Simons for years and, following the murder, she had also received angry phone calls from him.

"After JonBenet was killed," she told me, "Randy wrote a very strange article in a pageant newsletter saying that men in vans had come out to the small town where he lives and were going to get him if he didn't sell JonBenet's portfolio. He seemed paranoid about all this, and that's how he tried to justify selling her pictures. We gave him a lot of grief over that and he took it badly. We all have pictures of ourselves that we wouldn't want him to sell if we died."

Carol Hirata lived outside of Fort Collins and published *Stagelines,* the newsletter that contained Simons's "strange article" about being pursued by "paramilitary" types in the wake of the homicide. Hirata told me that she had also received calls from the photographer "at odd hours."

"He's handled the whole JonBenet thing in a very bizarre manner," she said. "He told me that his life was in danger and made some vague references about someone releasing inappropriate pictures of JonBenet if he didn't sell her portfolio."

LaDonna Griego owned the All Star Kids pageant, based in suburban Denver. Since January, Simons had made numerous disturbing late-night calls to her, yelling and crying and arguing with her if she challenged anything he said about the murder. He eventually became so distraught on the phone that she told him that if he ever bothered her like this again, she would contact the police. The calls ceased at once.

Simons shared with several of these women a couple of details he had not mentioned in the *Denver Post* article. One was that a week or so after the killing, a tabloid had offered him $15,000 for risqué pictures of JonBenet, such as a shot of her in her underwear or topless or nude. He said he did not have any pictures like that. The tabloids also promised him money under the table (meaning that Sygma Photo Agency would not receive a cut) if he would give them outtakes of JonBenet, in which her eyes were closed or she was making an ugly face. He told the women that he had refused this offer.

According to Pam Griffin and LaDonna Griego, Simons claimed that in the first week of January, when the case was generating great media interest and stories about the dead child were being prepared for a variety of magazines and TV shows, Sygma had put extreme pressure on him to sell Jon-Benet's portfolio. The New York distributor naturally wanted to cash in on this nationwide, if not worldwide, photo opportunity. Both women said that Simons told them that Sygma had given him an ultimatum: Hand over the pictures by midnight January 7, or the distributor would release photos of the girl that would embarrass everyone who knew her. It was at this point, Simons explained, that he caved in and relinquished the portfolio.

14

Representatives from Sygma refused to speak to a journalist about the company's business affairs, and calls to Randy Simons's Denver number and his eastern Colorado home did not produce results.

I phoned Alex Hunter to ask if his detectives had ever sat down with the photographer. In the first months of the case, the D.A. said, the police had briefly had contact with Simons, but his people had not. Hunter's own investigative unit now included Peter Hofstrom, a trial attorney who headed the felony division in the D.A.'s office; Hofstrom's assistant, Trip DeMuth; Detective Steve Ainsworth from the local sheriff's department; and, most significantly, sixty-two-year-old Lou Smit, a retired, highly respected homicide detective from Colorado Springs, who since March had devoted himself full time to the Ramsey matter.

Over more than three decades, Smit had built a reputation as a first-rate investigator who was especially good at working complicated killings and pursuing "cold" leads (in 136 cases, he had a 90 percent success rate). One of his most famous cases involved a man named Park Estep, who had attacked two Korean masseuses in Colorado Springs. After stabbing both women, Estep poured gasoline on them and set them on fire. One died, but the other survived and, from her hospital bed, was able to tell Smit that her assailant had driven a red truck. The detective began an indefatigable search for possible suspects while collecting photos of men who owned red trucks. During his visits to the hospital, he showed the survivor one picture after another, but none matched her recollection—until he showed her Estep's image. Shouting, she asked the investigator how he had ever found the man who had tried to kill her. Estep received a life sentence.

Like Alex Hunter, like Pam Griffin, and like virtually anyone else who took a public stand granting the Ramseys the presumption of innocence until proven guilty, Lou Smit soon came under attack for not quickly calling for the arrest of John and Patsy Ramsey. Rumors about Smit spread everywhere: His skills were wildly overrated, he was too old to investigate anything, he had deep religious convictions similar to Patsy Ramsey's and simply could not accept that a fellow Christian had done something so awful to her child. It was Lou Smit, people were saying, who was responsible for keeping Hunter from doing the right thing and filing charges against the parents.

Two days after I spoke with Hunter about Randy Simons, Pam Griffin told me about a photograph Simons had taken of her daughter. It showed Kristine with a kite Simons had made himself. Attached to the kite was a white, nylonlike material bearing some resemblance to the cord that had been tied around JonBenet's wrist. During one of Simons's panicky late-night calls to Griffin, he had asked her if she recognized the material on the girl's wrist. Although police photos of JonBenet's wrist had been published in the *Globe* in January

1997, Griffin could not answer Simons's query, she explained to me, because she could never bring herself to look at those pictures of the dead Ramsey girl. This admission made an impression on me, because Griffin was not a squeamish woman. The fact that for months this ex-nurse had been unable to view these relatively tame photos in the *Globe* indicated how much JonBenet's murder, and other violence against children, affected her.

After speaking with Hunter about the Simons photo, the D.A. asked me to get it from the Griffin residence and bring it to him so that his investigators could look at the nylonlike material on the kite and the handwriting on the back of the photograph. Later that day, I arrived at the Griffin home in a Boulder suburb, where Griffin lived with her husband, Jim, her daughter, Kristine, and three vivacious Pomeranians. The dogs gave me an extraordinary greeting. After peeling them from my body, I sat next to Griffin on her living room sofa and, at her request, placed the *Globe* issue in front of her, opening it to the pictures in question. While she studied them, I took in the room's huge television screen and one of Kristine's elaborate beauty crowns, laid out in a glass case.

"If someone we know on the pageant circuit was involved in this tragedy," Griffin said, laying the tabloid aside, "that would almost be worse than if John or Patsy had done it. We've trusted these people for years."

Before my arrival, Griffin had dug out the kite picture that Simons had taken of her daughter. With our amateur eyes, we tried to compare the material on the kite with the cord around JonBenet's lifeless wrist, but neither of us was qualified to make a reasonable judgment. As the dogs yapped at my cuffs, I thanked Griffin for letting me borrow this photo and left her home.

Half an hour later, Hunter came out to greet me in the lobby of the Boulder County Justice Center and I gave him the image of the kite. We walked back to his chambers and sat down. Two well-dressed men came in and introductions were made. One was Steve Ainsworth, the sheriff's investigator with whom Hunter had been consulting, and the other was Laurence "Trip" DeMuth, the attorney in the D.A.'s office who may eventually help prosecute the murder, if charges are ever filed. DeMuth was handsome and Ainsworth wore a gun. Both men looked exceedingly intense. They studied me with a tangible wariness, as if startled that Alex Hunter was actually taking information and potential evidence from a journalist. They seemed even more surprised when I mentioned Randy Simons, and they confessed that they did not know anything about him.

"Why," Ainsworth said, "would a successful photographer in Denver leave his wife and kids and move out to eastern Colorado? That's very strange."

DeMuth nodded.

They gazed at me with what I can only describe as extreme skepticism.

"We need to interview Simons," Hunter said. "Pronto."

"There are at least two people outside the Ramsey family," I said, "whose behavior has been interesting since the murder: Randy Simons and Fleet White."

The D.A. shot me a look, so I didn't go on.

Ainsworth frowned. DeMuth smiled at me indulgently, as if it were cute but annoying to have a Sherlock Holmes "wannabe" in Hunter's office.

Why had the D.A. just given me that look? Did he not want his people to know that he had been speaking freely with a journalist? Was I telling these men something they really had not heard before and were curious about? Or had they already looked into these things and dismissed them? Did they know far more about the photographer and the oil man than I was remotely aware of? Was the only reason they had allowed me into their sanctum sanctorum because I might be able to give them a scrap of information they had not yet discovered? Or were they simply clueless?

"Have you talked to Simons?" Hunter asked me.

"No," I said, describing how the photographer recorded odd messages on his answering machine, such as that he was "out in the yard right now but would be back in the house in ten minutes." I had tried to call him many times when I knew he was home, but he never picked up the phone.

Hunter walked over to his desk, which held the color picture of JonBenet in her pink sweater that had been on display before, and rummaged through some papers. He said that Lou Smit had been trying to reach Simons for the past couple of days, but that the eastern Colorado number I had given the D.A. wasn't working.

"You must have told it to me wrong," Hunter said to me.

I asked him if I could make a quick call from a phone in his office.

"Sure," he said.

I dialed Pam Griffin's home. When she answered, I asked her to check Simons's number against the ten digits I had for him in my pocket. She did this, and I thanked her and hung up.

"The numbers are right," I called across the room to Hunter.

DeMuth and Ainsworth, who had been watching all this with supreme concentration, began to laugh out loud. Hunter himself couldn't repress a smile.

"Wow," one of the younger men said, "that Lou Smit is a great detective, isn't he?"

"Yeah," the other replied. "He can't even get a phone number right."

"Boy, he's really something."

"Good ol' Lou's on top of it."

"All right, all right," Hunter said soberly, reaching for the phone on his desk.

He asked me to repeat the digits I had just gotten from Pam.

"I just want to verify that number," he said, dialing and then listening for a few moments in silence.

He suddenly dropped the receiver onto its cradle.

"Jesus Christ," he muttered.

"What is it?" Ainsworth asked.

"Randy answered," the D.A. said.

"He did?" DeMuth said.

Hunter's cheeks turned bright red. Pointing at me, he said, "I thought you told me he never picked up the phone."

"He never did before," I replied.

"Well, he did this time. I wasn't ready for that."

DeMuth and Ainsworth exchanged smiles. Hunter stood and gathered himself. I suppressed a grin. From the very start, the investigation had had a kind of bumbling, slapstick, all-too-human quality to it, in which everyone was trying very hard, yet basically stabbing in the dark. Nothing about the homicide, it seemed, was as obvious as it appeared to be and everything was slippery. The case was nearing one hundred and fifty days old, and I could not help wondering if the authorities were anywhere close to solving the murder.

DeMuth gave me a long stare, then excused himself and left. Ainsworth did the same, taking the kite photograph with him and checking it into the nearby "JonBenet Ramsey War Room," which held the eighteen thousand pages of material the murder had generated thus far (it would soon hold twelve thousand more).

When we were alone, Hunter said, "I didn't want to make too big a deal out of the Fleet White business in front of them, but his behavior still strikes me as bizarre. He keeps overreacting to things."

15

Departing Hunter's office, I walked out of the building and onto the bridge that spans the creek behind the Justice Center. By mid-May, water from the mountains was still rushing along its banks, carrying melted snow and ice through the heart of town. It was a clear, late afternoon and the sun had that fiercely brilliant quality that comes at this time of day at higher elevations in the west. Tree trunks rose black against the sun's rays. Leaf edges stood out against the sky. I stopped on the bridge and looked down at the stream, watching the water froth and the light play off its waves and swirls, realizing that it was this all-too-human quality that permeated not just the investigation of the murder, but the entire JonBenet phenomenon. In a curious way, nearly everyone seemed to be involved in the case—it had spawned thousands of sleuths on the Internet—just as perhaps, even more curiously, nearly everyone was connected to her death.

The more I got to know Alex Hunter, the more I saw him as a man in the middle of a hailstorm trying to find his way home. For twenty-five years, he had kept his tendencies and weaknesses as a prosecutor mostly out of public view. Now they were exposed not just locally but almost nightly on national television while his many career accomplishments were virtually ignored. The more I watched John and Patsy Ramsey, the more I sensed that while they were self-protective, defensive, and extremely frightened of the police, they were not the evil parents who had been portrayed in the tabloids. The more I talked to Jeff Shapiro, freelancer for the *Globe,* which for months had been depicting the Ramseys as wicked, the more I heard him say how deeply he wanted to do the right thing by avenging JonBenet's memory and bringing her killer—her mother—to justice. The more I listened to the cops' mounting frustration with the D.A.'s office, the more I felt that they were justified in their anger and were dealing with something they had never encountered before. And the more I tuned in to Peter Boyles and his early-morning radio sidekick, *Denver Post* columnist Chuck Green, the more I understood their motives as well. They were not acting out of spite in their continual desire to see the Ramseys held accountable; they were genuinely outraged that something terrible had happened in Boulder and were committed to speaking out against it.

All of these people had sensed a disturbance in the air, a feeling that something had gone haywire. This feeling, set in motion during O.J. Simpson's criminal trial, deepened with the Ramsey case. Hunter himself, not long after JonBenet's murder, had publicly said that the girl's death was providing his office with the opportunity to rebuild the faith in the American legal system that had been shattered by the debacle out in Los Angeles. But it hadn't done that, at least not thus far. Dr. Henry Lee's famous statement during the Simpson trial—"Something wrong"—echoed far beyond the walls of that courtroom and the details of those homicides.

The difficulty was not that people were upset and expressing their discontent. It was that they so desperately needed to put a single face on that disturbance—the face, for example, of Patsy Ramsey—as opposed to viewing the problem as anything larger than one individual or one crime. As brutal as it sounds, the murders of Nicole Brown Simpson, Ronald

Goldman, and JonBenet Ramsey were just three more statistics thrown on the heap of numbers that make up the annual homicides in America. Why did these deaths disturb us so much, when so many others didn't?

The obvious answer is because they received so much publicity. Yet the next question is: What has that publicity done to us? Has it frightened us badly because we are so afraid of being stabbed in the night or having our children taken away and killed? Has it angered us because we are being manipulated emotionally and physically by our most basic fears? Has it made us believe that one person was the source of our feelings, when the source was really much deeper? Has it made us look for someone to blame and punish—right now—so that we can get through our disturbance quickly and move on to other things? Has it made us stop cooperating with the principles of freedom of speech and our legal system? Aren't we just doing what humans do, which is to look for the fastest way to feel safe again? Is all this softening up our social underbelly for something worse?

These deaths are showing us just how easily we can be controlled and manipulated—and taught to hate.

I returned to my car and went for a drive around Boulder. At certain times, the town has the look and feel of a perfectly idyllic place. Streets are tree-lined. Large, attractive, red-brick houses fill the neighborhoods. You sense the presence of education, intelligence, and money. I stopped at a red light near the University of Colorado and saw handsome students pedaling up a hill toward classrooms or walking across the lawn carrying satchels and cups of coffee. Lawns held clusters of aspen or purple and yellow peonies. Young people rolled on the grass or tossed a frisbee to a dog.

Boulder breathes open-mindedness and political correctness. You can take community courses here in aromatherapy and rockclimbing for lesbians. You can find countless remedies for almost any bodily or emotional dysfunction, and in the summer of 1997, you could attend Hempstock, a festival that celebrated the plant's industrial uses and the soothing glories of the weed, sponsored by the eminently respectable Boulder County Commissioner Paul Danish. Two decades ago, Danish had devised the Danish Plan, which limited new housing in Boulder to 2 percent a year and added to the town's reputation as a progressive, enlightened place that took a stand against unrestricted development. You cannot overbuild in Boulder, you cannot smoke in public venues, and motorists are supposed to defer to bicyclists on the streets. Civility is expected to rule. Somebody in America is always conducting a survey about the best places to live in the country, and Boulder usually scores near the top.

I drove over to the deserted Ramsey home, very close to the campus. From the front, the Tudor-style structure was quite impressive, with handsome gables, dormered windows, and a subdued majesty in those old architectural bloodlines, but at the rear of the house, the Ramseys had grafted a half-million-dollar stucco rectangle onto the original floor plan. Part of it was invisible from the street, but if you craned your neck, the addition loomed near the alley—too awkward and too ugly to hide. The residence had been abandoned since the day John Ramsey had carried his daughter up from the basement, dead in his arms. Patsy Ramsey had not only vowed never to live in this "hellhole" again, she had kept her word. Children's toys were still scattered in the sideyard and the house gave off a tangibly lonely feeling, a complete emptiness, as if everyone had wanted to get as far away from it as possible.

I drove on to the construction site of the National Oceanic and Atmospheric Administration headquarters on South Broadway, a few blocks from the Ramsey home. I had heard numerous stories about this new federal building and wanted to see it for myself. A NOAA sign boldly read, BUILDING FOR THE PEOPLE—an insult to the three-thousand-plus local citizen-activists who had unsuccessfully spent years trying to stop the project. The site was located on a field that still held remnants of an ancient Arapaho medicine wheel, a circle of stones used for healing rituals and other ceremonies. The Native Americans who had once lived on this land believed that this patch of soil, which would one day become Boulder, was different from other locations, special, even sacred. Warring tribes that fought bitterly during the cold months came here in warm weather and lay down their weapons, camping side-by-side in the shadows of the Flatiron Mountains and renewing their strength so they could fight again.

This piece of ground, the Arapaho said, should be preserved as it had been created. Humans were only passing through, borrowing their bodies from the earth before returning to it. Tampering with this place was unwise, perhaps dangerous. For decades, Boulder had respected the ancient Arapaho wishes, but in recent years, the town had become more crowded and hurried, more expensive, and some of its charm had given way to "progress." The old medicine wheel would soon be crushed under the 330,000-square-foot NOAA headquarters, which would block some views of the Flatirons or even blot out the sun.

The desecration of this landscape, locals had been saying throughout the nineties, would only cause trouble, and trouble was now brewing in Boulder.

16

In mid-May I called on Ellis Armistead, the Ramseys' lead investigator. An Ansel Adams print adorned the lobby where he worked, but his office was as undecorated and unpretentious as the man himself. When Armistead had visited my home a few weeks earlier, he had appeared fresh and keenly alert, but now he looked weary and strained around the cheekbones. His six-foot-nine-inch body was sagging and his big shoulders sloped. He wore a bright yellow, short-sleeved shirt, which revealed an ugly red rash around his elbows. I wondered if he had been spending too many hours with his arms planted on his desk in downtown Denver, thinking about JonBenet's death.

"I wish I had your job," he said, smiling at me.

"You'll get over that," I told him. "Are you making progress on the case?"

He nodded vaguely, which was something he was good at.

"You look overworked," I said. "You must be putting in a lot of overtime on this homicide."

He frowned, as if his Ramsey timecard were not a proper topic of discussion.

"What are you focusing on, Ellis?"

In his southern drawl, which gave the word "case" two distinct syllables, he said, "Just solving the case. That's all I'm trying to do. Whatever success I've had in this field is because I listen to people who are a lot smarter than I am."

Some folks believed that Armistead's main task as the private investigator in this case was trying to learn more about potential suspects from a list of names the Ramseys had put together, a list that had thus far remained secret. Others felt that his real job was gathering dirt on Alex Hunter's office, which would be used by the Ramseys' lawyers against the D.A. if charges were brought against one or both of the parents. In recent weeks, the Ramseys periodically had made public pleas for citizens to come forward with any information that might be helpful in finding out who had killed their daughter. But did they really want to hear from outsiders?

"Are you getting many leads these days?" I asked.

"You have no idea," he grinned, "how many little old ladies in nursing homes have written to tell me they've solved this murder."

"That must be helpful."

He rolled his eyes. I gave him the same information about Internet child pornography that I had already told Hunter. Like the D.A., Armistead took notes. When I paused, he said that all of this was very interesting, again echoing Hunter, and needed to be explored in depth.

"Most people who come to me don't have any background in criminal investigations," he said in his most sincere voice, "but you do. This could be useful."

I asked if he were going to explore child pornography.

He nodded vaguely again.

I asked if he had heard of Randy Simons.

"No," he said.

I asked if he had looked into other local photographers who had taken JonBenet's picture.

"No," he said.

I asked if he were investigating child beauty pageants.

"No."

He had been writing furiously on a legal pad, but now he stopped and frowned again.

"What sorts of things are you investigating, Ellis?"

"Just . . . whatever we think may be important. Whatever may help solve the crime."

"Who do you think killed the child?"

He paused for several moments, as if he were thinking.

"We just don't know," he said.

I leaned back in my chair, put my hands behind my head, and gazed past him toward the wall. The air between us felt quite alive. The Ramsey case, at least to date, was not about events or facts or motives or witnesses or evidence, the way most crime stories were. It was about the feelings that were floating around this room, the nonresponses to questions, the fear and silence that were everywhere, the glances that you tried to interpret correctly, the blank space at the heart of the murder, and all the things that nobody wanted to talk about.

Something was coming off Armistead and moving across his desk and reaching me. It might have been frustration or annoyance, but it felt like anger.

"Do you and the Ramseys really want information about the case," I asked, "or is that all just public relations?"

"We really," he answered a bit testily, "want information. Do you have anything or are you just going to keep talking in circles?"

"The beauty pageants and photography issues might be worth looking into."

"I appreciate that," he said, offering an unfriendly smile.

"I hear that John Ramsey and Fleet White got into a big fight down in Georgia last December when they took Jon-Benet south to bury her."

His eyebrows moved but he didn't speak.

"Did you hear about that, Ellis?"

He shook his head.

"I hear the police had to come out because things got so heated."

He said nothing.

"I hear that the cops had to stay there for six hours, to keep the fight from escalating into something more serious. Six hours is a very long time, don't you think?"

He barely nodded.

"I wonder what they were fighting about."

He shook his head again.

"Isn't that a strange time to get into a nasty battle with your best friend?"

"What do you mean?"

"Your child is dead and you're facing grave legal trouble, maybe even a first-degree murder charge. You really need your friends at that time, don't you?"

"Yes," he said softly.

"Your best friends might offer all their support just then. That's what the Ramseys' others friends did and are still doing. What was the source of the conflict between the two men, Ellis?"

He glanced at the floor.

"I heard that the quarrel ended their relationship—permanently cut the families right off from one another. I heard they haven't spoken since. I even heard that John Ramsey wouldn't let the Whites fly back to Colorado from Georgia in the same plane as he and Patsy. Did you hear that?"

Armistead didn't speak.

"Just so you'll know, Ellis, I've told Alex Hunter everything I'm telling you about child pornography."

He leaned forward and placed his rashed elbows on his desk.

"What did Hunter say?" he asked.

"About the same thing you have. That this area needs to be examined by someone, but he can't get anyone to do that."

Armistead nodded.

"Do you think anyone really wants to solve this case, Ellis?"

"I do."

"You do?"

"We're doing what we can," he said, his voice again testy. "Nobody knows exactly what the truth is, and it takes times to get there."

"If you want to speak more openly in the future, give me a call. I can show you some staged Internet pictures of six-year-old girls being tied up, sexually abused, and tortured. They have belts and ropes around their necks."

"Okay," he mumbled.

I sensed that my welcome was growing thin. I was about to stand and say goodbye, but then he relaxed for the first time and told me a story about a local man who had enjoyed snapping pictures of bodies in the morgue. Armistead went into some detail about this fellow's grisly activities, and as he did, his unfailing politeness slipped away and the ex-cop revealed some of his old law-enforcement fervor. By the end of the tale, he was getting worked up.

"Anyone who would do that," he said of the photographer, "is a real sick fuck."

I shook his hand and left his office, thinking that regardless of what he was being paid for in the Ramsey case, he really liked solving crimes.

When I phoned Hunter and said that I had spoken to Armistead, the D.A. was extremely curious about our conversation and highly complimentary toward the investigator.

Armistead had a first-class reputation, Hunter pointed out, just like so many other Ramsey hires.

I told Hunter that Armistead and I had talked about the child pornography issue.

"How did he respond?" the D.A. asked.

"He just listened and revealed nothing about what he or anyone else on the Ramseys' side is doing."

"I understand that he's real good at his job."

"He's real good at keeping his mouth shut. He never says anything."

"Do you think he's investigating what you were talking about?"

"My impression is that the subject made him uncomfortable."

"That's very interesting."

During the next several weeks, I regularly called Hunter to discuss some recent local arrests for child molestation or Internet pornography, and to talk about a variety of photo scams involving girls and young women. There were stories of fashion or beauty-pageant photographers snapping pictures of youngsters while they were undressing and between outfits; talking girls into wearing no undergarments for modeling shoots because (the photographers said) those garments caused unsightly lines; asking if they could tickle a model's feet or legs in order to get just the right expression on her face; and demanding sex in return for taking pictures.

I had spoken with one man who had attended pornography sessions of teenage girls. He presented himself not as someone who wanted to have sex with the girls, which he seemed to regard as crude, but as a professional voyeur.

"My real interest," he had said, "is watching their faces and trying to figure out what the girls are feeling when their pictures are being taken. That's the turn-on for me, the mental part. Do they enjoy this work? Or are they suffering? Are they getting sexually aroused for the first time? Or are they bored? Are they still virgins or do they have some real experience? It's the psychological aspect of it that I find most fascinating. And seeing their raw innocence interact with the worldliness of the photographers."

17

As the spring progressed, so did the conflict between the Boulder D.A.'s office and the local police department. Since January 1997, the cops had had their own Ramsey team in place, with veteran detective Tom Wickman leading a group of five others: Tom Trujillo, Jane Harmer, Ron Gosage, Steve Thomas, and Melissa Hickman. The police resented the arrival of retired investigator Lou Smit three months into the case and felt that Hunter was trying to upstage them by bringing in a far more experienced murder detective than anyone on the police department's staff. Smit's hiring, went the scuttlebutt, just demonstrated the D.A.'s refusal to accept the Ramseys' guilt and signaled his desire to stall or bury the case. Smit's age, his religious convictions, and his relationship with Jesus Christ became running jokes at the police department.

Jeff Shapiro had struck up a friendship with Detective Steve Thomas. Periodically the *Globe* freelancer called me and passed along what he had heard down at the station.

"The cops don't like Hunter," he told me, "but it's that fuckin' Lou Smit who's the real problem."

"What's wrong with him?" I asked.

"He's a born-again Christian, just like Patsy Ramsey. He can't believe that good upstanding Christian parents would do this to their child, but these people are monsters who snuffed out their daughter's life. Smit's talking to Hunter and telling him all this bullshit about what fine people they are."

"Have you talked to Lou Smit?" I asked.

"No."

"Have you talked to people outside of Boulder about his reputation?"

"No."

"Do you know anything about him?"

"Just that he's fucking up the whole thing. Why are you in denial about the Ramseys' guilt?"

I did not respond.

"Is it because you're the father of a small child and you don't want to face what the Ramseys have done?"

"Could be," I said.

The police resented Hunter for reasons beyond what Lou Smit represented. In addition to the D.A.'s reputation as a soft prosecutor, the detectives knew that Hunter had long been allies with Democratic Party heavies in the area, like Hal Haddon, and that Hunter even had financial connections with William Gray, a business attorney for John Ramsey. These relationships raised charges of conflict of interest between Hunter and the Ramsey camp, charges that grew more serious when the D.A.'s office passed along reproductions of the ransom note and police reports on the case to the Ramseys' attorneys. To many people, this suggested at least the appearance of impropriety and reinforced their belief that Hunter was too badly compromised in these circumstances to carry out his duties as district attorney. The cops themselves made bitterly humorous references to their contention that D.A. employees were going to be "defense witnesses" when the Ramseys came to trial.

In summer 1997, as the anger was building between the district attorney's office and the police department, Ann Louise Bardach, a reporter for *Vanity Fair,* came to Boulder to gather information for an article for a fall issue. After getting her ears filled by unnamed "police sources," she went home and wrote a scalding article about both Hunter and Smit. She wrote about the "blunders and improprieties in the D.A.'s office"; about the cops calling Smit a "delusional old man"; about talk show host Peter Boyles saying that Hunter had "never met a criminal he thinks is fit for jail"; and about her own obvious feelings that the Ramseys appeared to be getting away with murder.

The police department had no choice but to accept the fact that Hunter wanted to work with outside notables like Barry Scheck, Dr. Henry Lee, and Lou Smit, but the cops adamantly refused to let the D.A. guide the homicide investigation. In many instances, police detectives and district-attorney gumshoes cooperate in the gathering of evidence—the district attorney making the ultimate decisions about how to proceed—but nothing about this case was standard. The cops could not understand why the D.A. did not want to pursue the Ramseys more aggressively, and Hunter was so frustrated with Police Commander John Eller that he once half-jokingly suggested to Jeff Shapiro that he do a story on Eller (this did not happen). Eller, who was inexperienced with homicide investigations, was determined to run this one his way, and his way, as Hunter had pointed out to me in his office, was directed straight at John and Patsy Ramsey.

The police agreed to share information with the D.A. once they had uncovered it, but they resisted Hunter or his people looking into things on their own. The D.A., however, felt that the police were deliberately avoiding areas that extended beyond the Ramseys and were not giving him everything they came up with—in part because they felt that he would inappropriately pass it on to the Ramseys' lawyers. By mid-1997, the most visible conflict in the case was not among any of the suspects, or even the lawyers, but between the police department and Hunter himself.

Under these conditions, what could the D.A. do? Whom could he turn to in order to further explore his own suspicions? The answer to the last question, I was beginning to understand—to my considerable amazement—was journalists. Hunter had told me to go find out more about child pornography on the Internet, a very difficult thing to accomplish without breaking the law; he had suggested to Jeff Shapiro that he snoop around John Andrew Ramsey's Chi Psi fraternity house and see if he could learn anything from the frat boys; and he had asked other reporters to keep him informed on their pursuits.

I had never heard of anything like this before, and a comparison with the O.J. Simpson case is revealing. In the initial two weeks after Nicole Brown Simpson and Ronald Goldman were murdered, Peter Bozanich, a first assistant to Los Angeles County District Attorney Gil Garcetti, told Garcetti to proceed slowly and be extremely leery of the evidence that had been collected against Simpson, particularly the bloody glove that Los Angeles Police Department detective Mark Fuhrman claimed to have found on O.J.'s property the morning after the killings.

Bozanich was quoted in the *Los Angeles Times* as having told Garcetti in the last week of June 1994: "There is something wrong with the glove. . . . What's it doing there [at Simpson's estate]? That doesn't make any sense. How did the glove get there? Was there any evidence of blood along the path? . . . There were no answers for me and by the time we got to trial, there were still no answers."

For his independence and courage in challenging the D.A.'s case against Simpson, and for his advice to exercise caution, Bozanich was soon transferred out of Garcetti's office and into the decidedly funky—some would say dangerous—Compton neighborhood.

He was not alone in his efforts. According to an Internal Affairs investigation conducted by the Los Angeles Police Department during the spring of 1995, two other lawyers in the D.A.'s office, Lucienne Coleman and Julie Sergojian, repeatedly tried to tell Simpson prosecutors William Hodgman and Marcia Clark that Mark Fuhrman had known Nicole Simpson, that he had neo-Nazi ties and was violently prejudiced against minorities, and that he was capable of manufacturing evidence. These women were ignored—to the point at which, the investigation concluded, "Coleman felt that [prosecutors] Hodgman and Clark did not handle the information she provided them in an ethical manner."

Throughout the Simpson case, journalists—myself included—attempted to inform the D.A.'s office that several things needed to be closely examined, but we were also brushed aside.

Three years later, the opposite was occurring in Boulder. Alex Hunter not only moved forward with extreme caution, he felt that the JonBenet murder investigation should be expanded beyond the inquiry conducted by the police. Most startling of all, he was asking reporters for help. It was not too difficult to imagine that more was going on in Boulder than had yet surfaced, but what could it be?

Even though I knew that Hunter was asking journalists to assist him, I was always surprised when he encouraged me to keep calling him. He was gracious on the phone, and I was struck repeatedly by his unfailing modesty and what seemed to me his basic decency and intelligence: He was flawlessly able to pick up the thread and remember the details of a conversation we had had a month earlier. I could only conclude that he had been paying some attention to what we were talking about and may have been pursuing it on his own.

The contrast between the bitter public criticism that portrayed Hunter as inept or something worse and my contact with him could not have been more dramatic. It was difficult to reconcile these two things, but not impossible. A complexity of the case that had not yet fully emerged was slowly leaking out of the investigation. For one thing, I learned that soon after JonBenet's death, word had reached Hunter from certain members of the Boulder political establishment that the situation was potentially explosive. Not only had a child been sexually assaulted and brutally murdered, but numerous powerful people had been in the Ramseys' home and had been exposed to JonBenet (the guest list for the Ramseys' December 23, 1996, Christmas party, held two days before the crime, was never released). The essence of the message to Hunter was simple: Be careful with this one. But what were they afraid of?

The complexity surrounding the homicide went deeper than the behavior of JonBenet's parents or their legal team or the police or Alex Hunter. It went to the evidence itself, some of which did not point to the parents. Among that evidence was DNA testing of dark fibers on JonBenet's labia that did not match anyone in her family, implying that the source of the fibers may not have been inside her home. Neither the white cord that had strangled her nor the duct tape on her mouth may have originated in her household, either. There were mixed genetic samples that were, at best, confusing and human DNA on her body that did not match her parents or younger brother. Other scientific evidence existed, which the talk show hosts knew nothing about—or perhaps didn't want to consider.

How did one fit all these things together? How could there be forensic information leading away from the Ramseys, coupled with parents who were not actively helping the Boulder Police Department solve the puzzle of who had killed their child? What if the crime scene were not the crime scene, and the crime itself very different from what the police had discovered at the Ramseys' residence on December 26, 1996?

"When I was hired by Alex Hunter in March 1997," Lou Smit once told me, after working on the Ramsey investigation for more than a year, "I thought this case was exactly what the media had been saying it was: a slam-dunk. I would be in Boulder for a few weeks, the murder would get solved, and I would go home. It just didn't happen that way.

"What the public has never understood or been willing to accept is that once you see the evidence in the case, you realize that this thing is extremely complicated. The media doesn't know what the evidence is. They think they do, but they don't. I do, because I've seen everything the police have collected, the thousands and thousands of pages of material, and I can tell you that it's a very complex case."

18

One day in late May when we were speaking on the telephone, Alex Hunter suggested something that would have been outrageous in any case. "Maybe you could persuade the tabloids to look into child porn," he said. "They're not afraid to spend money, and they can be much more aggressive than we can. They can bend the rules, but we have to follow protocol and that can be really frustrating."

For reasons that were unfathomable, Hunter could not get the right people to do what he wanted done in the most difficult and noted case of his life. So he was grasping for help from the tabloids.

I called Jeff Shapiro to discuss this option, but he only wanted to talk about his favorite subject: Patsy Ramsey's guilt.

"Hunter," he said, "is just confused or stalling for time because he doesn't want to arrest Patsy. Everyone knows she killed JonBenet and wrote the ransom note. She's a twisted bitch. Do you know what the 'S.B.T.C.' in the note stands for?"

"No."

"'Saved by the cross.'"

"I thought you believed it stood for 'Subic Bay Training Center,' where John Ramsey was stationed in the sixties."

"No. Not anymore. This was a religious killing. Patsy reads the Bible all the time and killed JonBenet for God."

"For God? I thought you believed that she killed her for bedwetting."

"She either killed her for wetting the bed or because of religious fanaticism or a combination of both things. It was definitely a ritual execution planned for Christmas night. I told the cops about this Bible verse, Psalm 118, which Patsy read constantly."

"How do you know that?"

"We just do. Psalm 118 goes like this, 'God is the Lord, which has shewed us light: bind the sacrifice with cords.' Doesn't that sound exactly like what she did to JonBenet? She bound her with a garotte and sacrificed her to God. The Bible was right by her bed the night of the crime. We think it was open to this verse. She probably read Psalm 118 just before the murder. She wanted to get caught so she left this clue behind.

"Patsy thinks the Bible wanted her to do this. It's the sickest thing I've ever seen. Because of Psalm 118, she put that figure of $118,000 in the ransom note. It's, like, she really wants to confess her sins to the world and be punished."

"I thought $118,000 almost matched John Ramsey's 1995 bonus at Access Graphics."

"Yeah, but Patsy wrote the note and we know she was referring to Psalm 118. Now she can't live with herself and is starting to crack up. She's a fuckin' nut case."

"How do you know she's cracking?"

"We have people watching her all the time. We have specialists working on this. You wouldn't believe what we have."

"If you're so certain that Patsy wrote the note, why can't the experts determine that once and for all?"

"They will, dude. I know they will. Just wait. I'm gonna go into the D.A.'s office and tell Hunter to get off his ass and do the right thing. I'm gonna make him listen to me. The cops love me and want me to do what they can't get done. So I'm gonna do that and be the hero."

I contacted some other more conventional media outlets about looking into Internet porn, but virtually everyone I knew in the press had already "convicted" the Ramseys or did not want to attempt anything beyond business as usual. Then I called John South of the *National Enquirer,* who had been in Boulder covering the case. He lived in Los Angeles on a houseboat and had been a tabloid journalist for more than two decades. Like many other reporters of his ilk, he was a workingclass fellow who had started his vocation in the United Kingdom, learning his trade on Fleet Street before coming to the United States. We agreed to have lunch at a delicatessen in Denver.

South didn't say much over the meal but mostly asked me questions about the case. Investigating child pornography seemed to interest him, and he said he would think about the proposition of our doing it together—I had some leads and he had resources—before giving me an answer. Sitting with him gave me a very peculiar feeling, something I had rarely felt before in any journalistic situation. Although he was quiet and reserved, I sensed that during the past twenty years he had been places and performed acts on the job that were not only outside my experience, but also beyond the boundaries of my imagination.

In trying to follow Hunter's suggestion, I laid out a strategy for South. It involved searching for connections to children other than JonBenet and it extended beyond Boulder. It was technically complex (because of the intricacies of the Internet), expensive, time-consuming, legally risky, and flew in the face of all the public theories about the crime. It would have taken hard work and commitment to produce any results, and it properly belonged in the realm of law enforcement. But Hunter had said give it a try. I never heard from John South again.

part three

The Summertime Blues

19

As the summer of 1997 approached, the situation in Boulder had taken on a comedic air. The police force voted "no confidence" in their chief, Tom Koby, and one cop in particular, Sergeant Larry Mason, decided to sue Commander John Eller for bad-mouthing him over some alleged leaks to the media. Linda Arndt, the first detective to arrive at the Ramseys' home on the morning of December 26, 1996, had been widely criticized for her handling of John and Patsy Ramsey that day. She was preparing to sue the city for distress, claiming that her professional reputation had been damaged. Other officers assigned to the Ramsey case were considering taking lie detector tests to back up their credibility.

Boulder's municipal government, which had long prided itself as a model of democracy, was undergoing a mini-revolt of its own—partly as a result of the unsolved murder. By the first week of June, City Manager Tim Honey was about to be dismissed, three of the nine city council members would soon be out of office, and Mayor Leslie Durgin was quitting her post. Tom Clark, the head of the Chamber of Commerce, was leaving his position, and neither Police Chief Tom Koby nor Police Commander John Eller were long for their jobs. Students at the University of Colorado had rioted over the right to drink without harassment by the police department, a plane had crashed at the outskirts of town, and a tornado had touched down near the city limits.

Was all this trouble befalling the community because of one small body in a basement? Or was JonBenet's death merely the catalyst?

Residents of Boulder had been in an increasingly bad mood before JonBenet was killed. A popular local bumper sticker from the early eighties proclaimed, DON'T CALIFORNI-CATE COLORADO. At that time, the phrase had been nothing more than a joke, but a decade later, as the defense industry downsized in Southern California, and as the Los Angeles real estate market broke, people began moving east. They were drawn to the hip, high-tech, medium-sized city of Boulder— a liberal, affluent college town right at the foot of a spectacular mountain range. Boulder was not only beautiful, it was politically well connected. Federal, state, and municipal dollars were everywhere. The National Center for Atmospheric Research, the National Oceanic and Atmospheric Administration, the Rocky Flats nuclear weapons plant, the University of Colorado, and the ever-growing county and city offices made the community what it was: a great place to be a Democrat with pork-barrel connections.

Southern Californians landed on Boulder with a thud. West Coasters moved in, ramped up the price of housing, clogged the streets, and gradually bent the city in the direction of suburban Los Angeles. Boulder spilled over its boundaries, and people began settling into the ugly condos that rose up along Highway 36 east of town, structures that evoked nothing so much as pastel tumors.

For decades, a balance of power had existed in the Boulder government among a hired city manager, a popularly elected city council, and the mayor, who sat on the council and was chosen by his or her peers. The mayor was often little more than another team player. There was always conflict, but there was also a lot of common ground: Virtually everyone in the local government was a Democrat and concerned with protecting Boulder's quaintness, its character, and its reputation as someplace special, better than other towns. Starting in 1959, the city voted to protect its still-pristine condition and regulate development, despite the best efforts of the builders and shakers who advocated more and more construction. This resistance lasted for thirty-six years, until 1995, when the community finally defeated a slow-growth amendment.

By the end of 1996, Boulder's citizens were arguing over several issues. Some were strongly opposed to building a 55,000-square-foot Safeway on the north end of town. Others were fiercely upset because they believed that Mayor Durgin had secretly helped the University of Colorado buy 308 acres in south Boulder for future development. The mayor's husband was a professor at the university, and she had close ties there. Boulder was known for its heated, freewheeling discussions about land use at city council meetings, but according to the Denver weekly *Westword,* the announcement of this purchase even "took city planners by surprise."

The old ways were disintegrating in Boulder, and the balance of power was shifting in the direction of the mayor. United States Representative David Skaggs, a Colorado Democrat from the district that included Boulder, had long been a backer of the new NOAA building, which had generated years of protest in town. Representative Skaggs and Mayor Durgin were very close.

Anne Fenerty, an activist who had fought the construction of the NOAA headquarters, believed that the structure was an unnecessary expenditure of public monies at a time when many people wanted to scale back.

"It became obvious," she wrote in a letter opposing the NOAA building, "that because of strong personal and political connections between Representative Skaggs and Mayor Durgin, there were not going to be effective negotiations to downsize the project."

In the early nineties, Tim Honey was hired as Boulder's city manager. Rumors constantly swirled around him and Mayor Durgin, but one thing was certain: The two were allies who looked out for one another and cared about each other's political future.

"Tim wanted to work with a strong mayor," recalled Sally Martin, a former city councilwoman who served under Durgin and Honey. "He built the throne and Leslie was only too anxious to sit on it. They were very close. She vacationed at his summer home back east, but I think their bond was more significant than anything physical. It was all about power."

"You can only be dishonest with the system for so long," said councilwoman Liza Morzel, "and then it can't withstand that kind of thing anymore. I've never seen any organization as dysfunctional as our city government became under Tim Honey and Leslie Durgin. Eventually, it had to collapse. All this turmoil we're experiencing now in local politics is good. What will come out of it is a complete re-examination of our city structure and how we can include our citizens in the process of running Boulder."

Until the Ramsey case broke, the local police department and municipal government were stable. Criticism of these agencies was subdued and contained. The fundamental notion that had long pervaded the town—protecting Boulder against the influence of the outside world, protecting Boulder's view of itself—had held firm, but now that, too, was changing. With the death of JonBenet and the fallout that was tumbling one official after another, people who had been waiting for years to chastise the power structure now had their chance.

"In recent times," said Duncan Campbell, a local attorney and the host of both radio and TV talk shows, "Boulder has gradually been taken over by the lords of the city—the mayor and her friends, the university, the real estate developers, the governmental bigwigs, the legal authorities, and the *Daily Camera*, the newspaper which services all of them and won't do anything to rock the boat. Boulder likes to think that it has a grassroots democracy, which it once did, but today we have a parody of that. The lords of the city care little for the public interest and are there only to help themselves and to not let any scandals get out of hand. That's the key thing to remember: Don't let any scandals get out of hand.

"In the Ramsey case, the corruption has finally come to the surface. The authorites have even stopped trying to keep up a facade of propriety. Alex Hunter, for God's sake, is in a real estate deal with William Gray, who works for the Ramseys. The Boulder cops have consulted on the JonBenet case with Robert Miller, another lawyer who's involved with Hal Haddon, the Ramseys' lead attorney. These people are all in bed together and all serving the notion that we have to protect Boulder and keep its nose clean. It's a total farce."

Lee Hill was a state and federal prosecutor in San Diego before moving to Boulder in the mid-nineties and becoming a private-practice attorney. In the fall of 1997, he unsuccessfully ran for the city council. One of his issues was the botched Ramsey investigation.

"During my campaign," he told me, "I pointed out that the JonBenet case exposes Boulder as a city in denial. It exemplifies the town's twisted self-image: Bad things aren't supposed to happen here, in our white, middle-and-upper-class community. This is Mork-and-Mindy land, and the laws aren't for us, but for the underclass. Our legal authorities have dissociated themselves in response to JonBenet's death. They don't want to look at it. They want it to go away. The only way the case will go away is by confronting it. But if Alex Hunter or anyone else really tries to confront it, they're up against the whole mentality that wants to preserve Boulder's reputation."

According to retired physician Robert McFarland, the town's legal attitudes are deeply rooted in local history. In 1951, the Atomic Energy Commission built Rocky Flats, a factory that turned out triggers for nuclear weapons, nine miles south of the city limits. Dow Chemical ran this installation, which provided work for more than two thousand people. In 1954, the National Bureau of Standards arrived in Boulder, employing 670 professional scientists and engineers. In 1960, hundreds more highly trained minds began working at the National Center for Atmospheric Research (NCAR). A Beech Aircraft division, a NASA spacecraft systems plant, and a huge IBM outpost also settled in town.

"I think the lack of prosecutorial aggression in Boulder," McFarland said, "has to do with the overwhelming influence of government here. You have federal employees all over the community, at NOAA and NCAR and other places. You have thousands of people working for the state at the University of Colorado and many others working for the city. With the Rocky Flats nuclear plant south of town, which has had plutonium and other radioactive materials on site, you had government spooks around here working in national security. Those people are often untouchable, in legal terms. This set the tone and created an environment in which you just didn't want to ask too many questions or take a hard look at anything. Now they need to look at something that may be larger than the death of one little girl and they're paralyzed."

Evan Ravitz had been named Boulder's Activist of the Year by the *Daily Camera*. "Boulder," he said, "used to be good at some social and political functions, but in recent years, the only thing it's been any good at is public relations. And as the Ramsey case has shown us, it isn't very good at that, either. The town isn't used to the kind of scrutiny it's been under lately and the strain is evident everywhere. One unsolved murder and things just start to unravel."

20

If prosecuting drug cases had always been a sensitive issue in Boulder, pornography and especially child pornography were even more sensitive. Careers could be destroyed and families shattered. Americans who had been exposed for sexual peccadilloes had been known to commit suicide. Our national desire for instant gratification was equalled only by our need to condemn and punish those who actually pursued such things.

One morning I spoke to the employee who had worked for the local government some years earlier, when pornography and sex toys were discovered in his desk. When he agreed to go into therapy, the matter stopped there.

Some Boulderites believed that Mayor Durgin had acted appropriately by giving this man another chance and not humiliating him or taking away his job. The very last thing the city had needed, they said, was the kind of negative publicity that such trouble could have generated. Others felt that by keeping this employee in place—but in a badly compromised position now—the mayor and her allies could wield more power than before. Everyone agreed on one thing: Sex was a very dangerous political subject.

I had not told this man why I was coming to see him, and for twenty minutes or so, we made polite conversation while he reviewed his background and considerable professional achievements. I had heard that he was extremely intelligent, articulate, and proud of what he had accomplished during his long career as a municipal civil servant. I found him to be all of those things, and charming as well. I did not relish the idea of questioning him about the only blemish on his record, but I had heard this story so many times and from so many different people that it was only fair to question him about it myself and give him the chance to respond in private.

When I asked if he had known any of the Ramseys, or ever visited their home, he said that he had never even been aware of the family until the murder. When I asked if he knew any of the Ramseys' close friends, he also replied no. When I asked if he knew the police detectives working the case, or the attorneys in the D.A.'s office investigating the crime, or some other government employees, he denied having contact with any of these people, before or after the killing. He had lived and worked in Boulder for almost two decades, and his last answer sounded hollow.

When I brought up the paraphernalia that had been found in his desk, he shifted in his chair and turned bright red. Speaking very slowly and carefully, he did not deny the event, but called it "a grotesque violation of my privacy." He repeatedly and emphatically stated that it had had no effect on his performance in office or on any decision he had ever made on the job.

"Some people believe that I was blackmailed back then by those in power in Boulder," he said, "but that never, ever happened."

Then he asked me what I intended to do with this information about his past.

I said I was not sure.

In a subtly pleading tone of voice, he asked me to handle it "with the greatest possible discretion."

"I have a family," he said. "That was a long time ago, and it's been over for many years. I'm sure you understand."

"Do you know anything," I asked, "about a pornography or child pornography ring operating in or around Boulder?"

He looked at me wide-eyed and said, "Yuuucck!"

"Is that a 'no'?"

"Yes, it is. I've never heard of anything like that. Is that what you're investigating?"

"Among other things."

"Have you found any evidence of it?"

"Perhaps. You don't know anyone involved in these kinds of activities?"

"No."

"And you weren't involved in them yourself?"

"No."

He gazed at me, his cheeks still red. He looked afraid and very vulnerable.

"Absolutely not," he said.

I had accomplished what I set out to. A few minutes later I shook his hand and drove back to Denver, rather impressed by the fact that he had not tried to convince me that the allegations raised against him were totally false. He had essentially confirmed what I had heard about him.

That evening, he called me on the pretense of clarifying a detail he had mentioned about his career. He then brought up the Ramsey case. It was obvious that he wanted to continue our talk. Again he asked me to exercise "great caution" with the information we had discussed and not to cause him any further hurt or embarrassment.

Then he said something unexpected. "Are you suggesting," he asked, "that JonBenet Ramsey was killed during a child pornography session?"

This question surprised me because I had not, in fact, suggested this during our meeting.

"It's a possibility," I said. "Why?"

"I was just wondering."

"Is it also what you're thinking?"

"I've only thought about it since this morning. No one else has said anything like that to me since this whole thing started."

I hesitated, to see if he would continue.

"I enjoyed speaking with you," he said. "That was the most enlightening conversation I've ever had about this case."

21

On the evening of June 3, 1997, Tim Honey resigned as Boulder's city manager. His resignation was only the latest in a series of events that had shaken the community and made people wonder what might happen next. Earlier that day, Alex Hunter had called me and wanted to talk. He sounded rather frantic. I happened to be in Boulder and immediately drove over to the Justice Center, where we retreated to his office. When we sat down, he asked me if I had learned anything new about the city official we had discussed a month or so earlier, the same man who would later call our conversation about the case "enlightening."

"No," I told the D.A.

"Have you decided," he said, "what you're going to do with that information?"

"Not yet."

"If the media got hold of that," he said, reiterating what he had told me before, only this time more forcefully, "it would look really bad for Boulder. We don't need that right now."

He stated this calmly, but with a seriousness and an intensity that I had never heard from him before. Many people had described to me the atmosphere of self-preservation that prevailed in the city—that of polishing and protecting Boulder's image as a great place for families, for business, for outdoor recreation, and for overall quality of life. Now I was experiencing it for myself.

Until that moment, I had resisted the thought that Hunter may have known or sensed (or feared) more about the crime than others in the local power structure, including the police. Something in his response to the murder *had* been mysterious and impenetrable, and had driven the cops to distraction. Something didn't quite add up. His past association with Hal Haddon had never been an adequate explanation for his willingness to share information with the Ramseys' lawyers and expose himself to the charge of being intimidated or even controlled by them. Maybe his office was sharing information because he wanted information in return, and this was the only way he could think of to get it. Bargaining with defense attorneys was certainly a more normal practice than sending out journalists to do your legwork for you.

Something subtle, it appeared, had made Hunter very hesitant to move forward with a prosecution until he was comfortable taking such action. He clearly was not comfortable yet, and even the suggestion of publicity surrounding a distant sex scandal now left him even more disconcerted.

Now he was asking me not to hurt his town any more than it had already been hurt, but he was doing so in a soft-spoken, delicate way. That seemed to be the way Hunter did many things, and it helped explain his behavior since the beginning of the Ramsey investigation. He was not going to place Boulder at risk, not until and unless he had a good reason to and could accomplish his prosecutorial goals. In these circumstances, he was not going to do anything lightly. He did not just work in Boulder, he lived there. He still had young children in the town.

This is not to say that Hunter was obstructing justice;

rather, he was weighing the consequences of questioning powerful people in depth about how a six-year-old girl in his community had been sexualized and abused to the point of death.

I told Hunter that I had recently been contacted by a woman who had seen a picture of JonBenet, months before the murder, in her parents' bedroom in their summer residence in Charlevoix, Michigan, during a tour of Charlevoix's finer homes. The photograph, the woman said, showed JonBenet with a provocative expression on her face, wearing nothing but make-up and a feather boa snaking around her torso. The woman was so taken aback by the image that she had gone home, called one of her relatives in Denver, and given a detailed account of what she had just seen.

While describing this incident to Hunter, I said, "Some photographers routinely ask parents if they can shoot their daughters nude. The answer, from what the beauty pageant moms tell me, is always no, but who knows?"

The D.A. nodded. "We've talked about this in the past."

"Risqué pictures of girls might even be used to promote a pageant career."

He nodded again. When I asked him if he was investigating Randy Simons or any of JonBenet's other photographers, he didn't want to talk about it.

"Do you know," I said, "exactly where JonBenet died?"

"We're still not sure about that."

"Are you convinced that she died in the basement?"

"We just don't know," he said vaguely.

"Are you convinced that she died inside the house?"

He paused, then answered, "To my knowledge, no one has suggested anything else."

"Does the evidence completely rule out the notion that she may have been killed some other place?"

"No, it doesn't."

I waited and then asked, "Do you believe that the Ramseys murdered their child?"

He was silent for a while, but it did not seem to me that he was avoiding the question. He was truly stumped.

"I've met Patsy," he said, "and she seems like a quality person to me. John . . . I don't know about."

"For the sake of argument," I said, "let's assume that the Ramseys are as diabolical as many people think they are. Let's assume that they killed their child and then wrote the ransom note. If they were committed to protecting themselves at all costs, why wouldn't John have gone outside and dropped the body a block or two away? Removing JonBenet from the house would have made their ransom note and their kidnapping ploy look a hundred times more credible. Why would two people work this hard to create a cover-up that makes them appear totally guilty?"

"You're forgetting that it was their child, their baby, and it was late December. Maybe they didn't want to put her out in the cold, even if she was dead."

We sat for a few moments without speaking.

"What if," I said, "they weren't working together?"

He glanced at me.

"What if only one of them knows what happened that night?"

Hunter said nothing.

22

Despite all the gossip and conjecture reported in the tabloids, nothing had yet established that either John or Patsy Ramsey had ever led an unorthodox spiritual or sexual existence. The opposite, in fact, appeared to be true. The most fascinating thing about the couple was not their unconventionality but their semblance of, in John Ramsey's words, "a normal American family that loves and values children, much like most of the families in this country."

In the two hundred days since the murder, no one who knew the Ramseys had stepped forward and offered any evidence of child abuse within the family or one credible anecdote about parental misbehavior. The Ramseys' friends, who were extensively interviewed following the killing, portrayed them as thoroughly regular folks. During his years as head of Access Graphics, John Ramsey had made some enemies, and after his daughter's death, a few of them had sniped at him in the media, claiming that he had treated them unfairly or was mean-spirited in business. A domestic employee or two who had worked inside the Ramseys' home had groused about some of the family's habits. But no one contended that the Ramseys had deviated from any sexual or social norm. The picture of them that came through most strongly was that they were almost the "people next door"—except for two notable things: They had far more money than most families, and they had groomed their young daughter, almost from infancy, to become Miss America and fulfill the dream her mother had never reached.

Patsy Ramsey grew up in Parkersburg, West Virginia, a town of thirty-four thousand on the Ohio River, the eldest of three daughters of Nedra and Donald Paugh, a Union Carbide engineer. Nedra, by all accounts, was a fireball, a force who wanted her daughters to have success and money, an openly ambitious mother who saw the pageant world as the doorway to those desires and pushed her girls in that direction.

As a sophomore in high school, Patsy was the first runner-up in the Miss Teen-Age West Virginia contest. Four years later, she decided to compete for the state crown, and after two more runner-up finishes, she captured that title. At West Virginia University, she joined a sorority, Alpha Xi Delta, made the dean's list, and took a degree in journalism. As Miss West Virginia, the green-eyed brunette was not flashy, but was known for her intelligence, compassion, charm, religious convictions, and down-to-earth manner. She had a rhetorical gift. During the 1977 Miss America pageant, she missed the final cut, but earned a talent award for her dramatic reading from *The Prime of Miss Jean Brodie.* Her sister, Pamela, also a brunette, was Miss Teen America in 1976; four years later, she represented West Virginia in Atlantic City, but also failed to win the Miss America crown.

In 1980, Patsy married John Ramsey, who was fourteen years her senior and had been married once before. He was born in Nebraska in 1943; when he was a teenager, his family moved to Okemos, a tiny village near Lansing, Michigan.

His father, a much-decorated transport pilot in World War II and the director of the Michigan Aeronautics Commission, gave his eldest son a love of airplanes and flying. As a high school student, John ran cross-country, played in the band, and learned how to operate aircraft. At Michigan State University, he was president of his fraternity and a member of the Reserve Officers Training Corps. In the late sixties, he served as a military pilot in the Philippines, after which he earned a masters degree in marketing. His career began as a salesman for an Atlanta electronics engineering firm, but he eventually formed his own business, Advanced Products Group, peddling computers, printers, and other high-tech items from his basement.

In 1988, the entrepreneur merged his company with two others to form the Boulder-based Access Graphics. Three years later, Lockheed Martin bought the business and named Ramsey president. In 1992, he moved his family from Atlanta to Colorado, where he would live through both his greatest successes and most nightmarish ordeals. In less than half a decade, Access Graphics grew from $150 million in sales to $1 billion, but soon after the family's arrival in Boulder, Ramsey's oldest daughter from his first marriage, Elizabeth, was killed in a car wreck in Chicago. Then in 1993, Patsy was diagnosed with ovarian cancer, and three years after that, JonBenet was murdered.

The Ramseys, who had been conventional college students, joined the most conventional organizations in Boulder. They were prominent members of St. John's Episcopal Church. Patsy was a standout at charity work for the Junior League, Opera Colorado, and the community hospital, while John was elected Boulder's "Entrepreneur of the Year" in 1995. By the end of 1996, they were the symbols of mainstream American success. The one visibly out-of-the-ordinary thing within their family was that they had spent thousands upon thousands of dollars on costumes and pageant lessons for their little girl, JonBenet, teaching her how to dress outlandishly, in sequins and long feathers, and how to bump-and-grind onstage like an adult woman when she was only six years old.

Following the murder, a portrait of the Ramseys' marriage gradually emerged, revealing some very conventional gender differences. Once Patsy had children, she became totally devoted to them, while John focused on expanding his business. If John were known for making money, Patsy was known for spending it. She not only poured lots of cash into pageant competitions, she also enjoyed giving lavish parties, once reportedly laying out $30,000 for a luncheon in Atlanta that was based on the theme of *Gone with the Wind,* for which she hired actors to play Rhett Butler and Scarlett O'Hara. After she was diagnosed with ovarian cancer, she became more deeply involved in her lifelong religious beliefs in order to prepare for death or, if possible, to help put the disease into remission.

Although John Ramsey faithfully supported his wife throughout her cancer treatment, there were reports that questioned his loyalty. In May 1997, Kim Ballard, a young woman from Tucson, Arizona, publicly claimed to have had three liaisons with Ramsey. In media appearances she said that she had placed an ad in *USA Today,* describing herself as a petite, blonde, Southern Belle seeking a professional man. Ballard said that John Ramsey contacted her and that they met in August or September 1994 at the Main Course restaurant in Tucson when John was in town on business.

According to Ballard, they met twice in Tucson and once in Denver, where they spent the night together at the Brown Palace Hotel. John Ramsey, as she described him, had good manners and "looked nice," but he also had a controlling personality and wanted to conduct their relationship on his terms. After three meetings, Ballard said, she ended the relationship because she was starting to get re-involved with her estranged husband. Following these media reports, she told the press that she had taken and passed a lie detector test regarding the validity of this information.

Other rumors about John and Patsy Ramsey had labeled them as hipsters whose sexual behaviors would make most of us blush. After learning that Patsy had been battling ovarian cancer since 1993, many people were willing to concede that this may not have been true about her, at least not anymore, but what about her husband? Didn't Kim Ballard's tattletale arrival on the media scene prove that he was nothing but a philanderer?

Under investigation by legal officials and reporters, Ballard's story fell apart. She was just another publicity seeker with something for sale. One afternoon following her story's collapse, on a whim I picked up the phone and called the *Rocky Mountain Oyster*, a Boulder sex rag, a kind of information clearinghouse for swingers around town. The *Oyster* (Rocky Mountain Oysters is a western term referring to bulls' testicles) carries all sorts of ads for the open-minded and the adventurous. I was curious to see if they had ever heard of John Ramsey before the tragedy or had any contact with him at their paper.

The answer was an emphatic, absolute no.

"Trust me," a woman at the *Oyster* said, "if we knew anything about that JonBenet situation, anything at all, we would have immediately called the police."

23

Although Patsy and her sister, Pamela, were attractive young women, neither had the classic southern beauty pageant look: blonde hair, blue eyes, and excellent features. JonBenet (with a little help from nature, in the dye department) had possessed all three. From early childhood, she exuded a physical potential that had eluded both her mother and aunt, a potential that was immediately realized in photos and pageant videos released after her death.

Publicly, Patsy had dismissed the idea that there was anything unusual about dressing her daughter in provocative grown-up clothing and entering her in beauty competitions. During the May 1 press conference, she had brushed aside the notion that the pageants could have had any negative effects on JonBenet's life and had seemed offended by the suggestion of a connection between the sexualizing of a very small girl and exploitation or predation by adults.

And yet, according to Pam Griffin, the evidence of the possibility of exploitation should have been clear to Patsy. She had seen risqué photos of young girls in Randy Simons's studio, and knew that well-respected photographers would shoot nudes in order to bolster portfolios and give girls a competitive edge. Wasn't it clear that the children—and their parents—would also benefit? After all, they were competing with thousands upon thousands of other youngsters. Simons was not the only professional employed by the Ramseys. David

Haskell, another Denver photographer, also took seductive pictures of young women; his promotional literature offered CD-ROMs with the titles, "Sexy Props," "Degeneration," "Nudes," and "Sex Sells."

There was nothing unusual about what Haskell was pitching to his clients. Sex did sell, and all across the United States, photographers were now peddling it while advertising the young women and men who used their services. That was how the game was played; it was normalized not only by the Ramseys, but by society as a whole.

In 1998, Michael Tracey, an Englishman who taught journalism at the University of Colorado, made a documentary entitled *JonBenet's America*. In it, Patsy again insisted that beauty pageants had not been that significant in her or her daughter's life. But John Ramsey said something different, and it seemed to take his wife by surprise, just as her remark at the May 1 press conference—about two people knowing what had happened to JonBenet because the killer had confided in someone—had appeared to surprise her husband. Had each of them stumbled on a truth with the cameras rolling?

John Ramsey told Tracey that the pageants *were* important to Patsy because she had had life-threatening cancer and might not live to see her little girl become a young woman and take part in the adult competitions. The implication was that Patsy's sickness had encouraged her to involve JonBenet in the pageants when she was still a child.

John Ramsey was exceedingly generous when it came to funding JonBenet's pageant activities. Yet, as Pam Griffin once said, he found the beauty pageant world "stupid" and its emphasis on a young female's physical qualities excessive. He may have been conflicted about letting his child participate in them, but he also did not want to interfere with what a potentially dying mother wanted the most for her only daughter. Who was he to deny his ill wife her pleasures and fantasies? Patsy might not be there to see JonBenet make her own run for Miss America, but wasn't it a comfort to her to know that the girl was well-launched on that path?

John Ramsey went along with his wife's plans until late 1996, when Patsy wanted to schedule a pageant appearance for JonBenet in Las Vegas. John said no. He didn't approve of his daughter parading around in a provocative costume in that city, a town full of gamblers and hustlers and who knows what? It was one thing to participate in pageants in a place like suburban Denver or Atlanta—conventional, middle-class cities, where things weren't supposed to go too far—but Vegas was different. Vegas was sleazy, maybe even dangerous. Vegas was out of the question.

Even if John Ramsey had not intervened, the trip to Vegas would have become a moot point, because by the time the pageant was held, in early January of the new year, JonBenet was dead.

After the murder, many people condemned the Ramseys for dressing JonBenet outrageously and entering her in beauty pageant competitions. Behind this judgment lay the presumption that child pageants reflected an underlying form of pedophilia, conscious or unconscious. There may be truth in this perception, but it was not the pageant people who became obsessed with JonBenet following her death. It was mainstream America—the media and culture—that could not get enough of her image or her story. The TV talk shows covered the case exhaustively, even when there was nothing remotely new to discuss. The same was true for radio, newspapers, and magazines. During 1997, seventy-four worldwide news agencies came to Denver to cover the Oklahoma City bombing trials of Timothy McVeigh and Terry Nichols. One hundred sixty such organizations have requested credentials to travel to Boulder should the JonBenet case ever reach the courtroom.

Over and over, I heard media personalities pose the same questions: Why is the Ramsey case creating such a stir? What makes it so intriguing? Why are we so drawn to this murder, instead of the others? No one seemed to have the answers.

Then in the late spring of 1997, Richard Goldstein, a writer for the *Village Voice,* authored a trio of articles about the rising sexualization and commercialization of children in the United States. Additionally, without accusing anyone of anything, he put JonBenet's death in a much larger social context: the process by which thousands upon thousands of young girls are now encouraged to become eroticized creatures long before they have any awareness of what is being done to them.

Although America has the highest rate of child homicides in the world, Goldstein noted, the public does not get that upset about the murder of a homely youngster. We respond much more strongly when the victim is an object of our desire. Combined with the horror we feel toward the death is the natural attraction we have for beautiful children. It is, however, far easier to acknowledge the former than to admit to the latter. The Ramsey case had touched and jangled our collective horrified libido, and we could not give it up.

Ironically, Goldstein wrote, child beauty pageants really began in the seventies, with the emergence of feminism. As women grew more powerful in the home and workplace, kiddie pageants flourished. Some men, who felt threatened by the rise of women, began looking toward younger girls for sex, and some women eagerly turned their daughters into miniature parodies of sex goddesses. Aspects of this phenomenon have surfaced not only in child pageants, but throughout the world of chic magazine advertising and books like David Hamilton's recent *Age of Innocence,* a collection of images of nude young girls.

The implicit message in these ads is that if you have tried everything else and still are not satisfied, you might want to consider teens, or pre-teens, as sexual material. The nymphet, a staple of American popular culture at least since the publication of Vladimir Nabokov's *Lolita* in the fifties, has gotten dramatically younger. The fictional Lolita was twelve. JonBenet was half that age at her death, and she had already strutted on stage like a Vegas showgirl. Tens of thousands of JonBenets are out there performing each weekend at suburban malls.

In the Shirley Temple films of the thirties, Goldstein pointed out, a father or paternal caretaker was usually the young girl's protector. Her antagonist was an outsider. Yet today, in example after example, we suspect the father (or mother) of the very worst things, even if there's no evidence to substantiate our feelings. Could it be that, in the absence of that evidence, uncomfortable feelings inside of ourselves are driving our thoughts about incest? Why are we obsessed with JonBenet's murder and so unphased by the deaths of thousands of other kids?

Many children, Goldstein concluded, exude erotic energy, and adults pick up on that. The more we deny our natural sensuality, the more it expresses itself in unnatural ways. "Only in a culture that represses the evidence of the senses," Goldstein stated, "could child pageantry grow into a $5-billion business without anyone noticing. Only in a nation of promiscuous puritans could it be a good career move to equip a six year old with bedroom eyes." And only in America, Goldstein added, could a child's precociousness be blamed not on our fascination with sexual children but on a father's incestuous actions.

"We are haunted by feelings that cannot be felt, and knowledge that cannot be known. Only when an awful deed is done do we realize that desire denied can become the killer inside."

24

By July 1997, an angry stillness had settled over Boulder. The city was losing its sense of innocence and moral certainty, its "wretched arrogance" or "terminal smugness," as some had labeled it. The mood was doubtful and glum. JonBenet's death hung in the air like the fading vibrations of a dissonant, unresolved chord that at any moment could burst into loud, ugly music.

No one seemed to know where the case was heading—or if it were heading anywhere. No one seemed to know for certain who had authored the bizarre ransom note, despite the growing chorus of pundits who accused Patsy Ramsey. She had scribbled it, went this theory, while her husband sat next to her and dictated the words. No one seemed to know if some much-anticipated DNA test results—on fingernail scrapings from JonBenet, on hair samples, and on blood found on the girl's clothing—had revealed anything of significance.

No one seemed to know precisely when or where the child had died, yet a few details had leaked out. The garotte had been made of white nylon cord and a broken artist's paintbrush handle (Patsy Ramsey was an amateur painter). A white blanket had covered the body as it lay in the basement, and the ligatures around JonBenet's neck and right wrist were very loose, which experts said was consistent with a staged crime scene. Later, it would be reported that four fibers from the dress Patsy Ramsey had worn on Christmas night were collected by forensic specialists from the sticky side of the duct tape that John Ramsey had ripped from his daughter's mouth when he found her body. Patsy had worn this clothing when she had put JonBenet to bed that night, and she had had it on the next day as she huddled over the corpse.

When the autopsy report was finally released in mid-summer, it set off gales of speculation and counter-speculation. John Meyer, the Boulder County coroner, had arrived at the Ramsey home at 8:00 P.M. on the evening of December 26, 1996, more than six hours after the body had been discovered, and he had only stayed there for ten minutes. From Meyer's report, we learned that JonBenet had been found in a long-sleeved white shirt embroidered with silver sequins in the shape of a star; long underwear; and white underpants with rosebuds and the word "Wednesday" on them (the Ramseys had told investigators that she had gone to bed that night wearing a red turtleneck pajama top, which was discovered in her bathroom sink). There were navy fuzzballs on her body, which detectives were still trying to match to a garment in the Ramseys' house. Her underpants and long underwear contained red marks and urine stains.

The autopsy was like everything else in the case: ambiguous. Following its appearance, some experts and other commentators rushed forward to say that JonBenet had been hit over the head with a hard object before she had been strangled to death with the garotte, but others contended that she had been asphyxiated first. Confusion also surrounded the report's revelations about the possibility of prior sexual abuse. Apparent markings on the inside of her vagina may have indicated *something*—but what? Who had made them and when and how? Was it a stranger or a family member or JonBenet herself? You could look at the evidence and draw any conclusion you desired, but did those conclusions take you any closer to her childhood reality?

By August, the only thing the public knew was that the older Ramsey children had been eliminated as suspects. Twenty-year-old John Andrew Ramsey and his twenty-five-year-old sister, Melinda, had been in Atlanta on the night of the crime. Burke Ramsey, who was nine when JonBenet died, had apparently also been dismissed as the killer. The best argument against him was not that he was too young to have fatally hit or strangled his little sister, but that he had been subsequently moved out of Colorado and sent to live with relatives in suburban Atlanta. It seemed inconceivable that if he were concealing horrific family secrets, his parents would have turned him loose more than a thousand miles away from their protection.

A fourth person, Fleet White, had been eliminated as a suspect as well, but conditionally: Hunter had only been willing to scratch him off the list based upon the current state of the evidence. If that state changed, the oil man's position could change as well. White was infuriated at being put in this kind of limbo and unleashed very hard feelings toward the district attorney. The oil man, determined to do something about his legal status, would eventually try to get Hunter removed from the case.

As part of his strategy, White befriended some of the cops who were working the homicide. He bitterly complained about Hunter's tactics to them, and to Detective Steve Thomas in particular. Thomas was in the original group of investigators assigned to the case by the Boulder Police Department. In his mid-thirties and with more than a decade on the force, Thomas was considered a polite, meticulous, and very professional officer. He was known for strongly identifying with crime victims. He was also known for taking cases, large or small, and pursuing them tirelessly, but his response to the murder of JonBenet Ramsey was beyond any tenaciousness he had displayed before. He was absolutely dedicated to seeing his version of justice rendered and made little attempt around reporters to hide his belief that the Ramseys were culpable. Early in the investigation, he identified Alex Hunter as an impediment to their arrest.

One journalist Thomas confided in was *Globe* freelancer Jeff Shapiro, who saw his role as more than mere confidant. "The cops are using me," Shapiro told me one summer morning, "to find out what's going on in the D.A.'s office. They don't trust Hunter so they've asked me talk to him and learn his secrets and bring them back to them. Isn't that awesome? A young tabloid reporter, a kid who's never even done this work before, comes to Boulder and starts doing this for the cops.

"I go to Hunter and he asks me what the police investigators are doing. I tell him they've already got the evidence to nail the Ramseys. Then I go to the cops and they ask me what Hunter is thinking. I tell them he's afraid of prosecuting the case and doesn't know what to do. Then I go back to Hunter and tell him what the cops are asking about him. I can't believe I'm doing this. I'm investigating the D.A. for the cops in the biggest case in Boulder's history. It's totally huge."

Steve Thomas and Fleet White found common ground in their view of Hunter. Thomas and other detectives viewed White as a friendly and important witness for the prosecution, if the case ever came to trial, since White had been with the Ramseys the night before the crime and the morning of December 26 and had accompanied John Ramsey to the basement when they had found the body. Although the cops felt that White's testimony could be crucial in getting a conviction against the Ramseys, they also worried that his treatment by Alex Hunter could turn the oil man against the prosecutors and into a hostile witness. Some of the detectives enjoyed sitting around the station and lambasting Hunter, so White's criticisms of the D.A. were quite welcome.

However, since the detectives were powerless to remove Hunter as an obstacle in their path, White began developing other options. One would involve Roy Romer, the governor of Colorado, another Democrat whom White would ask for assistance in getting rid of the D.A. and bringing in a special prosecutor.

While the oil man was building this strategy, Hunter was looking for unorthodox ways to investigate someone of whom he had been suspicious for months—in fact, ever since he had met him—a person whom at least some of the police officers did not want to investigate but believed should be fully cleared: Fleet White. Hunter's behavior only further infuriated White and Steve Thomas and cemented their bond.

Throughout the spring and summer of 1997, the Ramseys and their lawyers were not passive observers of these legal dynamics. They had gone on the offensive, first with the scathing letter Hal Haddon had written to Hunter and released to the media in late April, and then with the Ramseys' nationally televised press conference on May 1. According to rumors, the Ramsey team was putting together a list of suspects for the authorities, a list that reportedly included Fleet White.

In July and August, the Ramseys continued their attack by running a series of full-page advertisements in Boulder's Sunday *Camera*, asking local citizens to help them find their daughter's killer and soliciting leads about a suspect who had displayed "conflict with family" or "legal problems" or "financial stress," just before or after the murder. The ads sought to identify someone who had established "an obvious alibi" or been "very cooperative with the authorities," someone who had come up with "a legitimate reason to leave the area days or weeks after the crime," and someone who had been "extremely rigid, nervous, and preoccupied during general conversation."

The ads also showed fragments of the ransom note—the letters "M" and "W" and "r"—precisely as they had appeared in the two and a half pages found in the Ramseys' home on December 26, 1996. Did anyone out there, the ads asked, recognize this handwriting or have information about who may have penned the note? The ads also suggested that the killer might have been obsessed with "techno-crime" movies, because the note contained phrases similar to the dialogue featured in such films as *Dirty Harry, Ransom,* and *Speed.*

On the obvious level, the advertisements were part of the elaborate and expensive public relations campaign that had begun right after JonBenet's death. They were also aimed at potential local jurors, should the Ramseys go to trial. Yet the information in the ads was so general and so thin that many people—including veteran F.B.I. profilers, who were called upon to analyze the ads for the media—found them laughable. How many folks in the Denver-Boulder area had experienced financial stress or conflict with a relative during the last holiday season? How many had seen *Ransom* or *Speed*?

On a less obvious level, the ads revealed more than any previous statement delivered by the Ramseys during their two national TV appearances. The ads implied that the person responsible for the crime was not a complete stranger to the Ramseys, not an unknown intruder, but someone possibly familiar with their home, someone they may have known quite well and trusted. Why else would they seek information about a suspect with a definite alibi, a suspect who had been cooperative with the authorities, unless they were aware of someone who fit that description? Why else would they say that this person appeared rigid and nervous during conversation, unless they had seen that individual nervously engaged in discussions?

One morning I called Alex Hunter and asked what he thought of the ads.

"We think they're just a basic defense strategy," he said. "The Ramseys have to make it look like someone outside the family did this."

"Do you think the ads point to anyone in particular?"

"You mean someone close to the Ramseys?"

"Yes."

"You mean Mr. White?"

"Yes. He had an alibi for Christmas night because he was at home entertaining the Ramseys, and he was quite cooperative with the authorities, wasn't he?"

"Yes."

"He left Boulder soon after the crime for JonBenet's burial in Georgia."

"Yes, he did."

"Pam Griffin was an eyewitness to the events in the days right after the murder. She says that White appeared very rigid and nervous and controlling."

"Well, even if that's true, it doesn't make him guilty of anything."

"I'm not accusing him of anything, but the ads may be hinting at something."

There was a pause on the D.A.'s end of the line, and then he said, "An interesting thing happened when we talked to the two families."

"Which two?"

"The Ramseys and the Whites. In our interviews with the Ramseys, they indicated that they were very suspicious of Mr. White. But when we gave White the opportunity to say the same things about them, he didn't do that. That seemed strange to me, and I've never forgotten it. Why wouldn't he have pointed the finger at them, when everyone else is doing that?"

"What's the answer?"

"I don't know," Hunter said.

During the summer of 1997, Jeff Shapiro went up to Michigan to look for evidence that John Ramsey was a child molester. By now it had virtually been established that there was nothing to support this charge, but, according to Shapiro, "I had to do whatever I could to find *something* that showed John Ramsey was involved in this stuff."

Shapiro went; he dug and dug. He traveled around the state, he spoke to many people, and he plunged deeper into Ramsey's background than anyone else had. He found nothing, not one sliver of information to back up the allegations. His bosses told him to keep digging. While doing this work, Shapiro began for the first time to question his job. He felt a pang of conscience about pursuing John Ramsey in this way, feelings that would fester and nag at him when he returned to Boulder.

John Ramsey wasn't the only one the reporter was investigating. On several occasions, he had gone to Fleet White's home and tried to speak to him, but White had posted a sign telling the media to keep away and always told him to leave. The oil man was large, imposing, and fiercely protective of his privacy. He was also intimidating, the only person in Boulder forceful enough to frighten off the rising young tabloid star.

Yet Shapiro was not so frightened that he wouldn't slip over to White's house at night and peek in the windows or tail him in his car. Once when White realized that he was being followed, he suddenly turned his vehicle around, aimed it at the reporter, and began screaming.

"That scared the shit out of me," Shapiro later told me.

I decided to try my luck with White over the phone. I wanted to ask him about several matters and give him the chance to respond directly to some questions. Had he, for example, arrived at the Ramsey residence well before the banks opened on the morning of December 26, 1996, with twenty to thirty thousand dollars in cash, intending to make up a portion of the $118,000 in ransom money? If so, when had he been told to collect these funds, and where had they come from? Had he, as Pam Griffin had alleged, tried to keep people away from Patsy Ramsey in the days following the crime? If so, why? What did he think of the Ramseys' newspaper ads? And what had he and John Ramsey fought about down in Georgia? What was the source of their conflict? And why had he tried to get rid of Alex Hunter?

I left some messages for White, but they were not returned. When I finally managed to get him on the phone, he let me introduce myself before slamming down the receiver.

25

One summer noon I parked in front of a restaurant and walked inside. It was dark and full of piquant, spicy odors. I found a table in the rear and the waiter brought me some iced tea, which I drank slowly. I was waiting for someone I had avoided speaking with almost since JonBenet had been killed. A number of times I had promised myself that I was not going to call her, but after Jeff Shapiro had told me that he had become the go-between in the investigation between the Boulder Police Department and the D.A.'s office, I decided that this case was strange enough to warrant opening a couple of untouched doors. Besides, when in Boulder . . .

"Hello."

I glanced up and saw a large, gray-haired female standing in front of me, a worn leather bag draped over her shoulder.

"Hi," I said. "How are you?"

"Good," she smiled.

We looked at one another across the table, one of those odd stares that sometimes pass between people who are strangers, but who like each other for reasons that can't be explained.

I had met this woman in January in the Boulder Public Library during Police Chief Tom Koby's first nationally televised press conference about the murder. Koby had said almost nothing that evening, but following his speech, this woman had cornered me and delivered a passionate and haunting tirade. The authorities had no clue about this crime, she said, and if they were really serious about solving the homicide, they should turn to Boulder's greatest asset: the myriad healers, mystics, seekers, psychics, and others who claimed to have connections to the arcane, the invisible, and to those realms outside of normal human awareness. The city, she told me, was crowded with holy men from the local Buddhist temple; with peyote-soaked disciples who lived in the foothills; with Sikhs and Sufis who came home from work, took off their ties, and began to whirl; with seers and prophets and poets of bliss; and with shamans and witches who traipsed naked into the mountains at midnight, singing among the rocks and throwing bones into the fire.

"We have America's greatest collection of weirdos in this goddam place," she said, "and one of them can figure out this fucking mess before we all have a nervous breakdown. This murder will never be solved by the book. Ever. They have to start thinking about it differently."

She paused and asked, "But do you think they're going to listen to someone like me? An astrologer who associates with visionaries and lesbians? Never."

She had a point, if not a couple of them. Her town *was* crammed with vivid alternatives and characters.

"Look," she continued, "you seem pretty straight and grounded. Why don't you start looking in some new directions? Why don't you try something different? Maybe you could get some answers that way."

"Well . . ."

She phoned me two weeks later and repeated the same thing. And then the week after that.

I tried to ignore her entreaties, and for several months I

had pushed them aside, but after watching Boulder's legal system bumble and fumble, I found myself returning to her suggestion. The more I learned about the D.A.'s office, the police department, and the Ramseys' legal team, the more I asked myself if Boulder's New Agers could do any worse than the cops, the P.I.s, and the lawyers in this most peculiar investigation.

So, finally, I called her for lunch.

"I was really glad to hear from you," she said above some scratchy zydeco music after joining me at my table. "Reporters are so left-brained, so square and logical and predictable and limited. They don't even use the right side of their brain, where all the real mental powers reside. They think everything has to be proven, but the best experiences never can be."

"What do you mean?"

"Can you prove which of your intuitions was the most accurate? Or which orgasm was the most transcendent?"

I vaguely shrugged. These were not the sort of questions I usually confronted over a working meal. Perhaps it was time to get down to business.

"As an astrologer," I said, "what can you tell me about JonBenet Ramsey?"

"Very little, really. I just don't have enough information. I never met her or saw her hands. I never studied her lines. I don't know the exact time she was born on August 6, 1990. She's a Leo. Her birthdate suggests there was some tension inside her home between both the parents and siblings. It also says that this girl was going to be more famous in death than in life."

This last remark caused me to stifle a grunt. Of course she

would say that now, after journalists from all over the planet had trekked to Boulder and sent JonBenet's image around the world. In hindsight, anyone could see that the girl was going to become a celebrity from the grave. My interest in this kind of analysis began to waver.

"Her mother's a Capricorn," she said, "born on December 29, 1956. The trouble I detect in this kind of family is very typical stuff. Almost textbook. A controlling Capricorn mother and an outgoing, extroverted Leo child. There was bound to be conflict between them."

I took a sip of tea.

"There's a sexual sense to all this," she went on, "that's deeper than most people realize."

I set down the tea cup and stared at her. "What are you saying?"

"It's just something I'm picking up, but it's quite strong."

"I don't understand."

"JonBenet was probably not quite the passive little thing we would like to think she was in our sanitized middle-class minds. I know that's a horribly politically incorrect thing to say, but—"

"What?"

"Children learn what you teach them. And you can't always control everything they learn. She'd been encouraged to flirt and flaunt herself in front of boys and men and pageant judges. She'd been taught to wear certain expressions and to move in certain ways and to say certain things and . . ."

"And?"

"Women know about this stuff. About being suggestive in certain ways. It's a real southern thing, a beauty pageant thing, and her mother was a former Miss America contestant from West Virginia. And maybe—"

"Yeah?"

"There was more than one."

"One what?"

"One overstimulated male in her life. Get people stimulated and shit happens. My whole sense of the case is that we're looking at it too narrowly. We're too focused on the parents. Maybe it's more than a family crime. Maybe it's a social crime. Ask yourself this: What shuts up everyone? What paralyzes the system? What stops the Ramseys and their legal team from unraveling the mystery? What makes everyone look bad?"

26

In June, the Ramseys had left Colorado for their home in Michigan and then bought a house in suburban Atlanta, where they had lived for many years before moving west. They were reunited with Burke, who had been living in Georgia, and settled down not far from JonBenet's unmarked grave. John Ramsey continued running Access Graphics, but General Electric would soon purchase his company and ease him out of his job, shedding another piece of the family's past. Patsy and Burke began rekindling friendships with their former southern neighbors; Patsy had always felt more comfortable with Atlantans then with the northern Boulderites. Down in Georgia, the Ramseys' lives were relatively quiet and took on the facade of normalcy.

The biggest noise the Ramseys made all summer came when their lawyers vehemently denied that John or Patsy or their daughter had ever been involved in child pornography. In July, when it was revealed that the authorities had investigated the Ramseys' video collection and computer files for evidence of pornography—and come up empty-handed— Hal Haddon delivered another blistering rebuttal to Boulder's officials, which was released to the media.

"Any suggestion or hint by such persons," it read, "that John and Patsy Ramsey may somehow be connected with child pornography, and therefore implicated in the death of their daughter, is totally outrageous. . . . Boulder citizens and leaders should demand a professional investigation into the murder of JonBenet. If those who are in charge cannot conduct such an investigation, they should be replaced by professionals who can."

I agreed with Haddon. No child pornographer or pedophile would put a photograph of their little girl dressed in a feather boa in their bedroom for visitors to see as they toured their home. The picture indicated that the Ramseys were extraordinarily proud of their daughter—and just as extraordinarily unaware of what they were exposing her to.

By July, things had calmed down for photographer Randy Simons, so I was able to reach him by phone at his eastern Colorado farmhouse. In the spring, he said, when the Ramseys were heavily promoting the "intruder theory" to explain the murder, the authorities had investigated him. Yet, even when interviewing him, they mostly asked about Patsy Ramsey and her relationship with JonBenet. Simons told me that a recent *Globe* article, which reported that Patsy had been abusive toward her daughter during a lengthy photo session with him, was utterly false.

"When I was shooting pictures of JonBenet," he said, "she fell down once, but came up laughing. It wasn't like someone was torturing her. Patsy wasn't doing anything wrong. They just wrote it that way."

Simons angrily denied many of the stories that beauty pageant mothers had told about him the previous winter and spring, including the events surrounding the sale of his JonBenet portfolio to Sygma Photo Agency.

"That's bullshit," he said. "Sygma never threatened me. A lot of other people—mostly tabloid reporters—were coming to me and saying that risqué pictures existed and asking me if

I could get them some. I kept saying no, because I didn't know anything about that. They accused me of having them and that scared the hell out of me. I released JonBenet's portfolio to show what kind of pictures I'd taken, and how good they were. I was very proud of them."

Somewhat less defensively, he added, "The cops have talked to me and they may have come up with some pictures like that. I've also heard about some videos, and that her picture was on the Internet before she got killed, but I had nothing to do with any of this stuff. The police came out here and cleared me. Lou Smit personally informed me I have nothing to worry about."

Had he told Pam Griffin, I asked, that he did not have an alibi for last Christmas night, or was that a fabrication on her part?

"Yes, I did say that to her. I was at my farm out here alone, and I have a very good alibi up to a certain time, but they never released the time of death, so I didn't know if my alibi was completely good. That's very frustrating. I've offered hair and blood and handwriting samples to the police. I would cut off my goddam arm to solve this. Anyone who was ever considered a possible suspect in this case will live under a cloud for the rest of his life. I've worked with pageant girls for years, and after JonBenet was killed they've blamed people like me for what happened to her."

He hesitated and then said, "I live by myself and I guess I'm a little bit paranoid."

Why had he wept so much after JonBenet's death, and why had this gone on for weeks and then months after the murder, in a series of late-night outbursts to women who had never heard him cry about anything before?

"I was very upset that she was killed," he said. "I get involved with these kids. They come to me at ages three, four, and five. I get close to all of them. They're my kids. I steer them toward things like television commercials. I've photographed some of them for ten or fifteen years. They're all special to me."

With bitterness in his voice, he asked me why people thought it was unusual that he had become so emotional following the killing.

"A little girl got strangled," he said. "Don't you feel bad about that?"

"Yes, I do," I said, "but you seem obsessed."

He didn't respond immediately, and then he made a sound that resembled a man crying. The tears seemed a bit forced, but there was something real about them, too.

"Do you know more," I asked, "than you're telling me?"

"Of course I do. I have other things to say but . . . I'm not going to tell you. I don't have any first-hand knowledge of anything and I'm not a suspect in this case and I want people to understand that. I've been cleared."

Over the next several days, I kept thinking about Randy Simons. It occurred to me that he was perhaps one of the few people who could feel the tragedy of JonBenet's murder, instead of simply treating it as a curiosity or a news item, or of passing judgment on those whom he was certain had ended her life. He had actually met the girl and her mother, had talked to them, had watched them interact in positive ways. He had seen and heard JonBenet smiling and laughing in front of his camera, as opposed to the rest of us, who only knew her image and the media image of her mother.

Simons did seem genuinely touched by JonBenet's death, but his reaction to it remained unusual. He may have sensed something that he did not want to speak about, at least with me—an idea that met with great resistance from those involved with the pageant circuit: that his world of photography and child beauty contests had not only shaped part of JonBenet's existence, but may have played some role in her demise. That would have explained some of his tears and made it much harder for him to stop crying.

When I called Pam Griffin, she was busily sewing again, but this time she stopped and devoted herself to answering my questions. She was the kind of person who remembered more once she began talking, and sometimes she recalled events she had not even known were lurking in her memory. She now recollected that she and Patsy Ramsey had once visited Randy Simons's Denver studio and had seen on view a picture of an eleven-year-old girl, her shirt partially open in front.

"This photograph really bothered Patsy," Griffin said. "She seemed shocked by it and told me that it was inappropriate for a girl that age."

For months after the murder, the seamstress said, she had had almost no contact with Patsy, but had recently sent her a letter, via Access Graphics. In the letter, Griffin extended to Patsy the same invitation she had offered before.

"I told her that she knew who did this, but she needed to sit down and relax and really think about it. A lot of time had passed since JonBenet's death, and I felt she might be ready to try this. Sometimes in the past, before the murder, Patsy would show up at my house and just want to get away from everything and talk, either about her cancer or other things. That seemed to help her.

"My husband runs a beauty salon, and in the letter I told her she could go there and we would close down the business and lock the front door, so nobody would interrupt us or see her in there. We would give her a shampoo or do her nails or whatever she wanted. We would treat her like a queen, and she would have the chance to unwind and think and speak openly to me, like she used to. I thought this would be very good for her and she might remember something important about that night or the next day.

"I sent the letter off to Access Graphics, and a few weeks later, I spoke to Patsy. She asked me why I never wrote her anymore. I told her I had just written her a letter and described what was in it. She never got it."

"Why did that happen?" I said.

"I think her husband didn't want her to get the letter or do the kind of thing I was asking her to do."

"Why not?"

"I just don't know."

I began laying out for Griffin the kinds of things I had been exploring on the Internet and in some other places, and told her I had given this information to Alex Hunter over a period of months. She did not seem shocked by what I had learned about the graphic pictures of children that could now be found in cyberspace. She did not deny that something like this could have invaded not merely JonBenet Ramsey's life, but the child beauty pageant world itself. And she acknowledged that it even could have gone on without the parents' knowledge.

"When you talk to Mr. Hunter again," she said, "tell him that I'd be willing to put aside my personal feelings and queasiness in order to go on the Internet and search for pictures of other young girls in the Denver-Boulder area. I know what kids are on the circuit and who to look for. I don't want to see the kinds of pictures you're talking about, but I'll do anything to help resolve this tragedy."

I phoned Hunter and passed along Griffin's offer. Then he and I continued the pattern of our earlier conversations. I suggested some photos he might want to look for and he repeated what he had been saying since the spring: that he had very little forensic evidence to work with in this case; that no one would be arrested soon; that someone should explore the pornography angle, but that since he could not get the cops to do it, I should keep investigating. When I mentioned that I wanted to sit down with a computer expert such as Chuck Davis of the Colorado Bureau of Investigation, Hunter did not say he would help me. When I reminded him that downloading child porn was a felony for anyone but a legal official, he told me not to break the law.

His message, like so many other things about the case, was mixed, but not as mixed as others'.

I next called Ellis Armistead, the Ramseys' private investigator, in order to give him information. When he did not call back, I left some sharp comments on his answering machine. The Ramseys, I pointed out, were paying thousands upon thousands of dollars for ads seeking information about the case (not to mention what they were paying Armistead); why did they not want to speak to someone who was willing to share information with their P.I.—and who was asking for nothing in return? Armistead still didn't call me. Finally I phoned his machine and deposited an angry message, underlining the absurdity of the entire ad campaign and his role in it. I didn't expect to hear back from him.

Twenty minutes later, he called. He sounded sheepish and apologetic. Yes, of course, he was interested in talking to me, he said. He was always interested in learning more. He had just been very busy lately, but he absolutely wanted anything I could give him and was always open to new ideas and . . .

"Those ads," I said, "don't seem to me to be profiling a

nonexistent mystery man, or an unknown intruder who was walking around Boulder last December. They're talking about someone specific, aren't they?"

"Who's that?" he asked.

"I think you know who it is. Why don't you and I sit down and discuss what I've been looking into?"

"Well . . ." He gave the word two syllables. "We're pursuing other things right now."

"You're not really interested in pursuing this, are you?"

"Not at the moment."

"Call me when you're serious."

27

During the first half of 1997, most of the ransom note had been kept from public view—only pieces of it were released to the press—but as summer waned, more and more of it leaked out, until it was inevitable that all of it would appear in print. In late August it finally did. Nonexperts everywhere now had the chance to ponder over the mysterious two and a half pages, just as the professionals had been doing since late December 1996. It was a curious document, indeed. It said:

Mr. Ramsey, Listen carefully! We are a group of individuals that represent a small foreign faction. We respect your business but not the country that it serves. At this time we have your daughter in our possession. She is safe and unharmed, and if you want her to see 1997, you must follow our instructions to the letter. You will withdraw $118,000.00 from your account. $100,000 will be in $100 bills and the remaining $18,000 in $20 bills. Make sure that you bring an adequate size attache to the bank. When you get home you will put the money in a brown paper bag. I will call you between 8:00 and 10:00 A.M. tomorrow to instruct you on delivery. The delivery will be exhausting so I advise you to be rested. If we monitor you getting the money early, we might call you early to arrange an earlier delivery of the money and hence an earlier pickup of your daughter.

Any deviation of my instructions will result in the immediate execution of your daughter. You will also be denied her remains for proper burial. The two gentlemen watching over your daughter do not particularly like you so I advise you not to provoke them. Speaking to anyone about your situation such as Police, or F.B.I., etc., will result in your daughter being beheaded. If we catch you talking to a stray dog, she dies. If you alert bank authorities, she dies. If the money is in any way marked or tampered with, she dies. You will be scanned for electronic devices and if any are found, she dies. You can try to deceive us but be warned we are familiar with law enforcement countermeasures and tactics. You stand a 99% chance of killing your daughter if you try to outsmart us. Follow our instructions and you stand a 100% chance of getting her back. You and your family are under constant scrutiny as well as the authorities. Don't try to grow a brain, John. You are not the only fat cat around so don't think that killing will be difficult. Don't underestimate us, John. Use that good, southern common sense of yours. It's up to you now, John!

Victory!

S.B.T.C.

This had to be the only ransom demand in history that used the word "hence," or that contained a sentence with twenty-nine words, or that expressed concern about the note's recipient getting enough sleep before delivering money. It seemed to have been written by someone who was essentially nice but trying to sound nasty, someone who had never been in serious legal trouble before. The note was written to John Ramsey and the author appeared much more familiar with him than with his wife. The S.B.T.C. was widely believed to refer to the Subic Bay Training Center, where Ramsey had served in the military in 1968–69. The note teased Ramsey about growing a brain and being full of "good, southern common sense," which was odd because he was from Michigan. The figure of $118,000, which matched Ramsey's 1995 bonus from Access Graphics, was odder still. According to John Douglas, the former F.B.I. profiler whom the Ramseys had hired to interview them after the crime, that bonus money had gone directly into a 401K plan. Patsy had not even been aware of the transaction.

The note's handwriting started off shakily, as if the author were not quite sure how to proceed, but then it steadied and was smoother. After the document was made public, the talk show pundits continued their outcry: The writing looked like Patsy's, so she had obviously penned the note while her husband had stood by and dictated the words, after one or both of them had hit or molested their daughter and then strangled her, perhaps for religious reasons or because she had again wet the bed. These scenarios were clearly possibilities, but they also raised questions that were never adequately explained. Why wouldn't Patsy Ramsey have tried to disguise her handwriting more cleverly if she knew that the police would relentlessly scrutinize the note for clues to the authorship? Why would anyone have written so much if she were trying to conceal her hand?

But the most provocative questions were ignored in the public dialogue: What if someone had imitated Patsy's writing and had done a pretty fair job of it, a job that got better and better as the note progressed? Why should any of us assume that the note had only been written to throw off the authorities? For whom was it primarily intended? The cops, or someone else? Who would that someone be? If we could answer that question, could we start to understand why it was so long and rambling? And what hidden intricacies and treacheries of the heart, of two hearts really—John's and Patsy's—lay behind such a strange piece of writing?

Finally, what if the worst treacheries are sometimes inspired by the best of motives? What if the deepest betrayals are occasionally done for love?

28

After reading Richard Goldstein's *Village Voice* articles, I attended a child beauty pageant in suburban Denver. One middle-aged woman protested the event, carrying a placard saying that these activities were a form of child abuse, but none of the participants paid any attention to her, at least not to her face. Among themselves, they complained noisily that she had no concept of what they were doing.

"We're having fun with our daughters," one mother told me defiantly. "And's that all."

"We're teaching our kids about competition," another said, "because competition is what life's all about."

Before the pageant began, tiny girls, no more than two or three, walked the halls in full pageant regalia. They wore sparkling patent leather shoes, teased and ratted hair, or long blonde falls that streamed down their small backs. They wore layers of make-up and pink or white party gowns, heavy with frills and ornamental lace. They moved awkwardly in these clothes, looking like the figures on a wedding cake who had suddenly come alive. I was reminded of the powerful photographs of Diane Arbus, who had captured people in some of their most peculiar yet touching grotesqueries. You could feel the humanity of her figures—and your own.

The talent portion of the pageant began. A five year old, dressed as an American flag, sang and tapdanced to "Yankee

Doodle Dandy." A nine year old attempted to croon a sentimental ballad. Then the two and three year olds were marched out in front of us, while we stared up at them with perplexed expressions. For decades, show business careers had sprung from beginnings as humble as these, with mothers standing by and urging their children on. I was watching a tradition that may have commenced in vaudeville, but somehow these pageants weren't exactly vaudeville. Nor were they exactly entertaining.

While viewing the pageant, I was reminded of Surrealism, the artistic and literary movement that had begun in 1924 with the French poet André Breton. The American Heritage Dictionary defines Surrealism as a doctrine "proclaiming the radical transformation of all existing social, scientific, and philosophical values through the total liberation of the unconscious." Maybe by the nineties, the Surrealists had finally triumphed, and their exotic vision had become so ingrained and normalized in our daily lives that we had wandered into one of their paintings and were not even aware of it.

The unconscious seemed to be running amok. That is what I had felt watching Oprah Winfrey promote Mark Fuhrman's book on the O.J. Simpson case during one of her phenomenally popular afternoon TV shows. Oprah was the most important African-American in the national media and Mark Fuhrman was an ex-police officer in Los Angeles who had been accused in court of advocating rounding up African-Americans and burning them.

My perception of Surrealism deepened throughout 1998, as the White House media corps pounded President Clinton's press secretary, Mike McCurry, day after day to learn the things they breathlessly wanted to know: Had our reckless president kissed an intern? Had he had sex with her or ejaculated on her dress? A quarter-century after the zenith of American journalistic history, when the *Washington Post* had uncovered the Watergate scandal and helped topple the Nixon administration, the media had moved from tragedy to farce, from hard investigative work to mass titillation—and massive denial.

In 1997, Congress had outlawed some forms of pornography on the Internet. In 1998, independent prosecutor Kenneth Starr put what amounted to a publicly funded porn novel on the Net when he released a 445-page investigative document describing in detail the most salacious aspects of the president's relationship with former intern Monica Lewinsky. In the process of condemning Clinton, the president's critics lapped up every sexual detail in the Starr report and then spewed them out onto the airwaves. Our culture's basic quandary had only grown larger, deeper, and more malicious. We could use sex to promote or sell anything—razor blades, tires, or bottles of beer—but the act itself rendered us silly.

Surrealism was the mood at a party I attended one summer night in Boulder. The fine stench of marijuana floated thickly through the room and strobe lights flashed off the walls. Out on the small dance floor, body parts emerged and faded through the strobe, an arm here, a hip there, a nose flying through space. Someone danced on my toes—a woman with a feather in her hair. A man in bellbottoms spilled beer on my knee and gave me the peace sign, hoping I would smile back. The music was as loud and cutting as the first time I had heard it, nearly thirty years earlier. Jimi Hendrix was shouting about a love as entangled as crosstown traffic, his guitar line rising and falling and encoding the crazy loop of the American sixties.

The party was given by a middle-aged man, and the

theme was a celebration of the sixties, a nod to our recent past and its radical moments. It took place in a makeshift film studio whose walls were covered with Socialist and Communist theater posters from all over the Eastern bloc and the Soviet Union. They advertised plays by Bertolt Brecht, Sophocles, and Shakespeare. The artwork was brilliant, naive, and hopeful, capturing what people usually feel at the start of a revolution. The Soviet Union had collapsed, just as the sixties had at the end of that decade, but these posters were still very much alive.

Several tabloid reporters were clustered over in one corner, laughing and sucking in enough ganja to stoke an elephant. Some of them had begun their careers chasing after Princess Diana and her family in England. Then they were shipped off to Hollywood to run after movie stars, but by 1997, they had moved on to something new: They were now crime reporters covering the murder of JonBenet Ramsey. In many people's opinion, they were, in fact, now the main force pushing and shaping the coverage of this case.

They looked ecstactically happy to be at the party. Reporters could always tell themselves that covering the gruesome murder of a little girl was hell, but when the dope was flowing and the music was loud and the dance floor was hot, it could alter your whole view of tragedy. The scene was strangely reminiscent of the sixties in Vietnam, where some young American journalists had gone to report on a guerilla war that they hated—and gotten higher on blood and pot and Jimi Hendrix singing in the rice paddies than they would ever get again. Nothing is more addictive than violence.

I wandered over to one of the tabbies, a foreigner, and asked how he liked the upscale, image-conscious town of Boulder, Colorado.

He cleared his throat and replied, "I must say that we

haven't been very well received here. This place is so damned stiff."

An American standing next to him put it a little more succinctly.

"Who the fuck," he chuckled, "do these people think they are? They're no better than anyone else we go after and destroy."

A couple of other reporters joined these two and they all began trading war stories. They howled about Jay Elowsky, a local restaurateur and the Ramseys' friend, who had gone after a pair of civilians with a baseball bat, convinced they were tabloid journalists. Elowsky had badly scared the poor fellows and had been arrested for his efforts.

They screeched about the tabloid photographer who was stationed out at Denver International Airport last winter, when John Andrew Ramsey flew in to see his family. The cameraman's job was to approach the college student and ask, "How does it feel to know that your father fucked your step-sister and then killed her?" The goal behind the question was to get John Andrew to take a poke at the photographer, who would then snap his picture in mid-swing. When this image appeared in the tabloid, it would illustrate to readers just how dangerous and out of control the Ramseys really were.

The tabbies guffawed about the drugs John and Patsy had given nine-year-old Burke right after the murder, to keep his memories of JonBenet's last evening on earth a blur. The men were funny and witty; they could make you laugh whether you wanted to or not. While smoking and joking, they revealed a few of their impressive bundle of tricks: bugging people's homes and capturing intimate conversations; calling up interview subjects and telling them that they worked for *The New York Times;* writing untraceable checks to the secret lovers of famous people, who then tattled to the tabs; and the old ruse known as "flushing"—telling someone they had illicit pictures when they really didn't—which then caused that person to produce and sell risqué photos of his or her own.

Another ploy was cutting up and pasting pictures together so that it looked like certain people were together when they really weren't. Another was using computers to manufacture images. Another was writing articles and faxing them off to the individual they were covering, or his or her lawyer. That person was given exactly fifteen minutes to deny everything in the story, and if he or she did not do that in writing, the tabs took this as confirmation of the article's accuracy.

Another was making up quotes. Another was breaking into people's houses and taking a look around. Another was illegally obtaining credit card records, through the use of hackers who went into mainframe computers and siphoned off financial information. And another, of course, was spreading around some guerrilla journalism.

Although my request to John South of the *National Enquirer* to help investigate child pornography had gone nowhere, by the fall South had struck up a close acquaintanceship with one of Patsy Ramsey's longtime friends, Judith Phillips. Phillips, who had moved to Boulder from Atlanta, lived several blocks from the Ramseys' abandoned home, right next to the residence of Stephen Miles, a middle-aged gay man who lived with his ninety-year-old mother on the upstairs floor of a modest house. Some years earlier, Miles had taken an artistically rendered nude photo of a seventeen-year-old male with his hands covering his genitals, which later appeared in *Aperture* magazine. Although the image was not explicit, it led to Miles's arrest, because the young man it depicted was under eighteen. The police seized two thousand other pictures from Miles, none of which were incriminating. The case did not go to trial, and the photographer was never convicted of child pornography or any other sexual offense including pedophelia.

According to Miles, one afternoon in the autumn of 1997, he was out in his sideyard doing something he very much enjoyed: attending his elaborate cactus garden. Judith Phillips walked over and asked him if she could talk to him, indicating that it was very important. He went next door and John South was there. South told him that in the upcoming *Enquirer,* the Ramsey camp would say that Stephen Miles was the leading suspect in the killing of their daughter.

Miles was stunned. He had never been interviewed by the police or even remotely connected to the case. He claimed that he asked South if he could read what had been written about him, and South complied. Miles became upset and said that it was full of inaccuracies—the main one identifying him as a pedophile—and that the publication of the story would damage his life, his mother's life, and his lifelong relationships in Boulder. South, Miles alleged, pulled out twenty $100 bills and waved them in his face. If Miles would simply take the money for exclusivity rights with the *Enquirer,* he was told, the tabloid would run another article the following week clearing up all the mistakes. Miles refused. He says he was then offered another $2,000 and given precisely fifteen minutes to decide whether to take the cash and go along with the story. He refused again and the article ran, with a picture of him resembling a mug shot on the cover.

After the story appeared, somebody slashed Miles's tires and put dead plants on his porch. He eventually sued John Ramsey, John South, and the *National Enquirer* for defamation of character.

* * *

I drifted away from the tabloid group and looked around the room, feeling a wave of nostalgia for the sixties, perhaps the same wave everyone in middle age feels for his or her youth. Although the party's theme was appropriate in this setting—because Boulder viewed itself as an outpost for that decade, a place where a fragment of revolt and social protest remained—that time was long since dead.

What had made the sixties unique was that people realized that something different was happening and nobody knew what it was. But that was all right—we would figure it out later. A little chaos would not kill us. A new idea or two would not bring us down. We had not yet become a generation (and a nation) that desperately needed to fill up the unknown with easy opinions and with everything we were afraid of. It was all right to have a few mysteries. For a moment or two, we got to investigate our reality and explore and experiment, to make mistakes and accept that that is how you learn. Cynicism was not yet rampant and we could still be surprised.

In the sixties, not knowing was perceived as an asset instead of a liability, because not knowing led to discovery and vitality and creativity. Not knowing had driven Jimi Hendrix to teach himself how to play music; you could feel his defiance and his love and joy parting the air inside that studio nearly three decades later.

For a while, I just stood there listening to Hendrix and letting his pleasure blow through me and rattle my skin. Something in the high notes, in the speed of his fingers and the yelp of his guitar, was the very opposite of stupid and unfree—and the miracle was that this sound could still give you hope and freshen your blood. It could empty you of judgment and remind your heart of something and someone you adored. It could shove aside blame and see the entangled beauty in combat or even in death. It was a slash of red music across the sky or a blue note bending toward the sun.

I left the party and walked outside and looked up at the stars above the Rockies. A startling drumbeat poured from an open window and men's laughter followed closely behind it. I leaned on a fencepost and searched in the darkness for the big yellow moon. It was halfway up over Boulder.

29

One evening, Ellis Armistead called, sounding like a changed man. He had reached an important decision: He wanted to work with me on the child pornography angle. He had been thinking it over and was ready to take this seriously. It was time for us to sit down and develop a plan.

"That's good," I told him on the phone, feeling a bit like a schoolgirl who thinks that the handsome boy asking her out might be pulling a cruel prank. "You really want to do this, Ellis?"

"Yes. How do we proceed?"

"Well," I said, not completely reassured, "I think you and I should go talk to some people. Confront them face-to-face. They don't like journalists, but if you're with me, we might be able to do more than either one of us could do alone. I'm sure you know tricks and maneuvers I've never thought of."

"Oh," he drawled, "it's not really like that."

The investigation, I said, would have to include pornographic material on the Internet. Pam Griffin had volunteered to go online and look for illicit pictures of local kids, and Armistead himself, I suggested, could figure out how to get around the legal difficulties of downloading child porn.

"Do these activities interest you?" I asked him.

"Yes," he said, "they do."

Then he began asking me about the interest in child pornography taken by Alex Hunter and the Boulder Police

Department, and any names associated with child pornography that I had uncovered in the area. He was friendlier with me than he had ever been, and while he had come across as sincere in our earlier conversations, he now oozed the stuff. We talked for an hour, or rather I talked mostly and he listened, just as we had always done. I knew that he was wringing me out again, but that was all right. I treated him the same way I treated Hunter: I gave him parts of what I had, curious to see what he would do next.

He finally said that he was tired and had to go. He really appreciated my openness and cooperation, and he would call me the following morning or afternoon, when we would plan the initial phase of our investigation.

He did not call the next day or the day after that or the following week. When I phoned him, he did not return my calls. I left a message or two for him, but there was not any point in scolding him again on his answering machine, no point in expending the energy. He had been totally consistent with me from the start: He had never done what he said he was going to do, had taken all he could and given nothing in return, and had then disappeared back into the smokescreen that characterized the Ramsey team's investigative methods.

One day I phoned a veteran private investigator in Denver and described my interactions with Armistead.

"Based on your experience," I asked this man, "what do you think happened?"

"It's hard to say," he told me, "but if he was willing to call you and give you that kind of time, I think he was interested in your information. After talking with you, he went to the people above him and asked them what to do with it. They must have said, 'Back off.'"

If Alex Hunter wouldn't take action and if Ellis Armistead couldn't, maybe somebody else would listen.

30

By the summer of 1997, Detective Sergeant Tom Wickman had put in almost two decades with the Boulder Police Department. One evening early in his career, while was responding to an on-duty call, he got caught in the high winds that occasionally sweep down from the Flatirons and tear through Boulder. Locally, they're known as chinooks. This one picked up Wickman's patrol car, slammed it against a light pole, and snapped it in half, just behind the driver's seat. Only Wickman's pelvis was fractured, but he could have been killed.

After recuperating, Wickman returned to the force. In recent years he had served under Police Commander John Eller. His ex-wife, Linda, was employed by the district attorney's office, so he was intimately aware of the inner workings of Boulder's legal system and familiar with both its prominent and behind-the-scenes players. Now the detective himself had become a lead investigator of the Ramsey homicide. Tall, blond, and broad-shouldered, he conjured up the straightest of arrows. Many people around town, including ex-police officers, said that Wickman was just what he appeared to be: an honest cop who had always put himself on the line for the public.

Wickman agreed to meet with me at the police station one Friday afternoon in July. The moment I sat down with him at a conference table in a small private room, he said that he would hear me out, but that he was in the middle of an unresolved case and could share nothing with me, nothing at all. I expected him to give me twenty polite minutes, thank me for driving to Boulder, and steer me toward the door. By now, rumors that the murder investigation was winding down and the police work was essentially finished were circulating around town. Patsy Ramsey would be arrested soon, or perhaps Patsy and John both. If these rumors were true, it was unlikely that Wickman would pay any attention to what a stranger had to say.

Wickman had a soft voice and a gentle manner, yet on a couple of occasions he looked as if he wanted to leap up from his chair, pound the table, and shout out his frustration over the Ramsey case (I had heard that this was exactly what the Boulder police had done more than once, while hurling expletives, during this most unusual investigation). But he just sat very quietly and stared at me, clenching his teeth and holding his fire.

"I wish," he said on a couple of occasions, "I could tell you some things and go further with you, but I can't. Maybe in the future I'll be able to, but right now, I just can't."

I began talking. Fifteen minutes passed, then thirty, then forty-five, then an hour, and then an hour and a quarter. For whatever reason, Wickman let me speak while he leaned back in his chair and took in the information, sometimes smiling or making affirmative gestures, sometimes scribbling on his pad. His behavior mirrored the earlier actions of the district attorney and Ellis Armistead: Wickman wanted everything I had and offered very little himself.

I told him a story that afternoon. It was part-factual, part-conjecture, and was based on some things I had been thinking about almost since the murder had occurred. It was the same story that I had given Alex Hunter and would later give to his investigator, Lou Smit, the same story that I had partially laid out for Ellis Armistead, the Ramseys' lead private investigator. I engaged in this speculation with Wickman not because I was convinced that the story was true, but because I wanted to offer an alternative scenario to Patsy Ramsey's guilt and get a visible, physical response from someone who did not seem to have any agenda other than solving the case. I wanted to see whether he would dismiss the story out of hand.

"Most men," I said, "love their wives and want them to have the things they desire. Sometimes, husbands will go to great lengths to achieve this, particularly if they feel something is important to the person they've married.

"Many women want their children, and their daughters in particular, to achieve the things they never did, by becoming lawyers or scientists or even, perhaps, Miss America. But it takes years and years of preparation and work to earn that title and in some instances, the mothers might not be around to see their daughters reach their goals.

"If a man believed that he could help his wife and daughter fulfill their dreams, he might be inclined to try to nudge those dreams forward. If he learned that certain kinds of photographs—promotional photographs, let's say—were useful in assisting this process or boosting a career, he might agree to have some taken of his child, especially if he'd been assured that everyone else was doing this now, and it was perfectly safe and innocent and harmless.

"An event gets set up involving a 'special' photographer on a 'special' night. The whole thing will only take an hour or so and then it will be over. There's nothing criminal about it and nothing wrong with this kind of thing. It's perfectly normal nowadays, people have told him. Nobody needs to know about it except for those involved, not even his wife, because she'd just worry and make a fuss. So the child is removed from her house, and from her parents, for this seemingly innocent purpose."

Wickman gazed at me and touched the point of his chin, completely silent and completely expressionless.

"She arrives back home dead," I said. "Something happened, a stupid little thing went wrong and before you knew it . . . it was an accident, just an accident. . . .

"The man is now confronted with two very serious problems: his wife, who is upstairs sleeping, and the police. At the moment, his wife is undeniably the biggest one."

Wickman made a movement in his chair. I thought he was going to speak, but he didn't.

"Do you have children?" I asked him.

"Yes," he replied.

"When I take my little boy to the park, and he falls down and scrapes his knee, I'm a little reluctant to bring him home."

The detective smiled an understanding smile.

"Because," I said, "my wife is going to hold me responsible for what happened, whether I'm at fault or not, because I failed to protect our child."

"Yes," he said, chuckling.

"Sometimes, you try to soften the reality of things for people you love."

He nodded.

"In these excruciating circumstances, the man needs a strategy—fast. The only handwriting most of us are familiar with, other than our own, is our spouse's, and we could always find samples of it lying around the house."

I paused, waiting for Wickman to shake his head and tell

me, as the media had been doing with certainty throughout the year, that Patsy Ramsey was the only serious contender for authorship of the ransom note. Wickman held his silence. Perhaps he, like the F.B.I., the Secret Service, the Colorado Bureau of Investigation, and an unnamed private firm in California—all of whom had been asked by the Boulder authorities to examine the note—had not been able to reach a definite conclusion.

Boulder's officials would soon hire another expert, Donald Foster, a Vassar College linguistics professor, to study the document. Foster would eventually write a long report on the matter, concluding that Patsy Ramsey had penned the note, but there were two significant difficulties with his analysis. The first was that Foster had approached the Ramseys' lawyers months before he began working for the Boulder authorities, and they had turned him down. According to Pat Furman, one of the Ramseys' attorneys, Foster wrote a letter to Patsy Ramsey on June 18, 1997, which read: "I know you are innocent—know it absolutely and unequivocally. I will stake my professional reputation on it, indeed my faith in humanity." The letter went on to say that he felt Patsy "did not write it and the police are wasting their time by trying to prove that you did."

The second difficulty was just as major. When Foster later changed his mind and told Boulder's officials that he thought Patsy had written it, he focused not on the handwriting per se, but on three other areas: certain words, indentations, and punctuations commonly found in Patsy's scribblings (she was fond of exclamation marks, for example). All of these things, of course, are easy to imitate. Finally, and perhaps most importantly, Foster was inclined to believe that John Ramsey had probably dictated the note, because its content sounded more like his mind at work than his wife's. There were eleven books in the Ramsey house that may have been source material for the note, and John had read at least seven of them, far more than Patsy had.

Anyone who had ever studied John Ramsey's handwriting from contracts or other documents could see that it was very creative and fluid, much more so than his spouse's. Wasn't it just a small jump from there to the possibility that he had written the note alone? Had he written such a long note not necessarily to fool the police—which in an accidental death might not have been his first concern—but to convince Patsy of its authenticity? And to protect her from parts of the tragedy—while protecting himself from her wrath? Had he written this particular note in order to frighten her to such a degree that she would never question its reality? Who knows better than a husband what his wife is afraid of and how to push the panic buttons? Didn't she understand from pieces of writing inside their own home that people really did abduct youngsters from families and do terrible things to them in basements?

No one ever knows in advance when and where the next media circus will explode. So who could imagine ahead of time that by jotting down some words on a legal pad, perhaps half of the people in the United States would come to believe that the person you were closest to on earth would now be perceived as a child killer? One could speculate further that unconscious motives were at work here; that a husband was deeply angry with his wife for leading their daughter into a world he had never approved of; that some of that anger had filtered out into his actions . . . and he had set his spouse up for a vicious public attack.

* * *

I was still waiting for Wickman to contradict my scenario, but he had said nothing.

"A man's greatest ally in this crisis situation," I went on, "is going to be his wife's emotions. He knows her habits well. He knows that she'll find the piece of writing at the foot of the stairs when she goes down early the next morning to make coffee. He knows that she'll become hysterical and dial 911. When the police arrive, he knows that she'll overwhelm them with her grief and tears. He knows that they'll be distracted by the power and sincerity of her feelings. Because of her, they might really believe a child has been kidnapped. At least for a while."

I looked across the table and again waited for Wickman to respond, but he hesitated.

"That," he said, "is very interesting."

He offered nothing more.

"While the police are distracted and confused," I said, "the man manages to find the body and ruin part of the evidence. The plan is working perfectly. His wife knows nothing and the cops have bungled the case beyond his greatest expectations. But two days later, something goes wrong. The police will not give him back his child for burial, because they know that the death was not an accident but a murder, and they've decided that he and his wife are the only logical suspects. It's at this point that the worm, as the man says months later on television, turns. That clearly means that despite whatever he may have thought earlier, he now knows that he's in deep trouble.

"He begins surrounding himself with lawyers. Two for him and two for his wife, because there's a potential conflict of interest between them, because they don't know exactly the same things or have exactly the same legal liabilities. He also hires a public relations expert to tell people what to think and feel about him and his family, but even an expensive P.R. rep can't make a body in the basement look good, so after a while, the flack is let go."

I paused again, staring at Wickman. He spoke in the form of a riddle.

"Everything in this case," he said, "is not as it seems. I can tell you that, but I will not elaborate."

"Months pass and the man decides to run a series of ads in the newspaper. They hold a very subtle and secretive message. This crime wasn't committed by a stranger or an intruder, they say, but by someone his family knows, someone who did something with his child. It's something he doesn't want to talk about and something that could open up doors that might be very uncomfortable not just for himself or his family—but for Boulder as well. Prominent people could get hurt."

The room fell still. I had had my say and decided not to continue unless Wickman gave some feedback.

Slowly, and with extreme caution, he said, "That is very incisive. I know how the political game is played around here. A few years ago, I was investigating something and got close to a city council member. They pulled me off the case and put me back in a patrol car on the street. That's how things work in the real world.

"Despite all that, I really want to know what happened in the Ramsey case. I intend to solve it and I don't care who gets hurt in the process. We're going to get the answers—no matter who goes down."

"Maybe," I said, "there are just too many political barriers to get the case resolved. Maybe the D.A. doesn't want to hurt certain people, unless there's some very good reason to do that. And he can't find one, at least not yet."

"I've had my suspicions about the D.A.'s office for a long

time," Wickman said. "You should have come to me months ago, instead of taking your information to them. I think some of their behavior has been inappropriate."

"Like what?"

"Talking too much, especially with reporters. You should have come to us."

"Why is it," I said, "that people want everything to be very simple and clean? We want investigations to be perfectly efficient and for the obvious suspects to be the bad guys and for them to get caught quickly and then be tried and convicted and punished."

"Every cop thinks the same way," he said. "They want to solve crimes immediately and have the obvious people be guilty. That's just the way we live now. Get it done and move on to the next thing."

"What if there's nothing simple or clean here? What if a good parent and a good man inadvertently participated in his child's death because he was trying, in his own way, to express his love for his wife?"

He nodded.

"What if he really doesn't know what happened that night or who killed the girl?"

He nodded again.

"What if he's divided against himself in the deepest corners of his being? What if he wants to know and doesn't want to know at the same time? What if he wants a father's revenge but feels so guilty that he can't do anything to get that revenge? What if his heart is broken, but he can't talk about that with anyone, not even his wife?"

Wickman nodded once more and said, "The public and the media don't really know what's going on."

His tone of voice was slightly different and more open than before. "What do you mean?" I asked.

"It's like in the O.J. Simpson case. People don't really know what happened out in Los Angeles."

I gazed at him. "What are you saying?"

He glanced away, as if he had just entered uncharted territory for a police officer, and was not sure he should have done that with a civilian.

"It wasn't a murder like people think it was," he said.

"How do you know that?"

"I just do."

I leaned forward. "Then what was it?"

He shook his head.

"What was it, Detective Wickman?"

He shook his head more firmly.

part four

Waiting

31

In late August 1997, I called Alex Hunter about some local men who had just been arrested for soliciting kids for sex on the Internet or downloading child pornography. Recently, in the Denver metropolitan area, teachers, photographers, and religious figures were arrested for illicit erotic activity with minors, some of it computer related. (A picture of JonBenet would soon turn up in the Columbus, Ohio, home of James Partin, who had been arrested for distributing child porn on the Internet; Partin was also under scrutiny in the 1983 disappearance of fourteen-year-old Beth Miller of Idaho Springs, Colorado.) Hunter asked me to find out the names of the police officers had who arrested the men and of the attorneys who were now representing them.

I told the D.A. about my recent meeting with Detective Sergeant Wickman. He became very attentive and asked if we had discussed child porn. When I said we had, he was eager to know everything we had talked about. In the past, I had never detected any anger from Hunter, but near the end of our conversation, he heatedly stated his belief that the police had uncovered evidence of child pornography, but had not shared it with him because they no longer trusted the D.A.'s office.

"The cops are guarding what they've done in this area," he said. "I don't think they've gone into the kind of depth in child pornography that they should. Their focus is more on the family and at the incest level. Some people working on the investigation have made up their minds it's the Ramseys, but I haven't. Keep looking into child pornography and let me know what you find. I'd like to investigate it more myself, but there isn't a helluva lot of support for that around here right now."

For weeks, the papers had been filled with stories about the significance of an upcoming trip that several Boulder officials, including Wickman, Hunter, and Lou Smit, were about to make to F.B.I. headquarters in Quantico, Virginia, on September 8–9. They were to speak with experts in the Child Abuse and Serial Killer Unit, and speculation was high that this gathering would help bring the case to some resolution and a possible arrest. The D.A. and the cops were finally reaching out to those who had deeper experience in investigating complex murders than they had, and, just as importantly, they were doing it as a team. The squabbling that had characterized some of their earlier interaction appeared to be behind them now, and things were at last moving forward.

Three days after my talk with the D.A., Hunter spoke to Tom Wickman. No TV or newspaper reports revealed what took place between them, but from later published accounts, I learned the result of their meeting.

"Conversations Hunter had Friday with the F.B.I. and with Boulder Detective Sergeant Tom Wickman," the *Rocky Mountain News* reported on August 31, 1997, "caused him to cancel on joining them for the trip to Quantico."

One could only guess at why Hunter had decided not to go. Had the subject of child pornography uncomfortably surfaced between the men? Had Wickman confronted Hunter for his loose-tongued behavior with journalists or his evidence-sharing with the Ramsey legal team? Had Hunter accused him of withholding valuable information from the

D.A.'s office? Or had the trip to Quantico simply not been worth the effort for Hunter, because the F.B.I. couldn't provide any magical solutions to the case and the D.A. knew that the investigation was nowhere near a conclusion?

The cops went to Quantico and came back committed to looking at and eliminating possible sex offender suspects in the Boulder and Denver areas. They went through eight hundred of them.

The same day that the *Rocky Mountain News* story appeared about Hunter's canceled trip, something happened halfway around the world that echoed the tragedy of JonBenet's death on an international scale. Diana, the Princess of Wales, the most photographed woman on earth, was killed in a car wreck in Paris. Initial news bulletins said that paparazzi on motorcycles had been chasing the Mercedes the princess was traveling in and were trying to snap her picture when the vehicle crashed inside a tunnel, ending three lives. Reports estimated that the car had been going at about 100 miles per hour. Some people blamed the accident on the paparazzi and their tabloid employers; others on the Mercedes' driver, who was legally drunk; and still others on Princess Diana herself, for staying up late and partying with the fast crowd.

The explosion of feeling that followed Diana's demise seemed disproportionate to the event itself. She was, to be sure, the most famous woman on the planet, yet nobody could have predicted the global outpouring of grief or the countless bouquets of flowers that arrived in London to mark her passing. People from many different nations spent tens of millions of dollars on floral arrangments to say goodbye to someone they had never really known, except as an image on television or a picture in a newspaper or magazine. In the three months following Diana's death, British psychiatric clinics noted that admissions of mental cases dropped by 50 percent, and doctors at the clinics interpreted this to mean that the release of England's legendary repressed emotions following the car crash had been a very good and cathartic experience for those throughout the United Kingdom.

Was the world mourning something larger than one untimely death? It was difficult not to conclude that the global consumption in the press of Diana's image and emotions, and her minutely chronicled marital problems, had all laid the foundation for her demise in an automobile wreck in France. Did it really matter exactly who was responsible for the crash? An entangled, interdependent world of economic, psychological, and social needs had put her in the circumstances that had extinguished her life. Some of those needs belonged to her alone, some to the paparazzi, and some to the rest of us, who had spent years buying and selling her image. If we did not know *who* had killed her, it was fairly obvious *what* had done the job.

Like the photographer Randy Simons in eastern Colorado who had cried for months after JonBenet's murder, millions of people stared at Diana's coffin on television and wept. We sensed that something was wrong and that we were involved in it, even though we could not quite give it a name. A month after the publication of Carlton Smith's *Death of a Little Princess,* the first book published about the Ramsey case, a real princess was dead.

Three nights after the car crash, actress Fran Drescher condemned the role of the tabloids in Diana's death on the *Larry King Live* TV show and severely pummeled another guest on the program, *Globe* editor Tony Frost. During the show, Patsy Ramsey phoned in and blasted Frost too, denouncing him for publishing JonBenet's crime-scene pictures and his coverage of the girl's murder. Patsy called for a boycott of all tabloids. She became so livid, her voice began to crack. She had recently taken her son, Burke, to a suburban Atlanta store to buy back-to-school supplies. At the checkout stand he saw a headline proclaiming that his parents had killed his little sister.

"These are trash!" she said of the tabloids.

Patsy Ramsey's grief and sorrow seemed real, her indignation genuine. Yet once again, she did not acknowledge that she herself had devoted years and countless dollars to promoting her own daughter's face and small body so that one day she might become a celebrity—the very sort of person who sooner or later ends up in the tabloids. Once again, Patsy had avoided recognizing her own involvement in the sexualization of a young child.

On the air, Patsy compared Diana with JonBenet, whom she referred to as "America's people's princess." It was an oddly revealing statement, perhaps taking us as close to the core of JonBenet's life, and her death, as we have yet come. Patsy seemed unaware that her daughter had never been a princess anywhere except inside her own family; she certainly had not been one for the American masses. She was just a six-year-old child, almost completely unknown before her death, who had been brutally murdered. She was a kid who would never grow up.

32

In October, Police Chief Tom Koby announced that he was taking Commander John Eller off the Ramsey investigation and replacing him with a veteran officer named Mark Beckner, a solid, modest, diligent man who listed among his qualifications the ability to get along, and cooperate, with Alex Hunter.

Beckner held his first press conference as the new head of the Ramsey investigation on December 5, 1997. He stood at a podium in front of scores of media personnel, with eight solemn-looking detectives—including Tom Wickman—fanned out behind him. Nearly all of them had been laboring on the case, day and night, for the past eleven months. Beckner said very little that day and his arrival had no immediate obvious effect, except for one thing: The news leaks surrounding the investigation from the beginning now slowed down.

The cops wanted the D.A. to communicate with them instead of journalists, and Hunter had complied, summmarily bouncing Jeff Shapiro out of his office and ending his role as a "go-between" for the authorities. Almost a year after the murder, the police and the district attorney were finally starting to work together.

Throughout the end of 1997 and on into the new year, Hunter slowly tried to rebuild the credibility many felt his office had lost since the case had begun. As part of that strategy, he used the tough-minded, tough-looking, outspoken suburban Denver D.A., Bob Grant of Adams County, to appear on many national TV programs and to talk about the investigation. Grant was effective and unintimidated by any reporter, lawyer, or talk show host who threw aspersions at the Boulder authorities. He seemed to enjoy verbal combat as much as Hunter shied away from it. Hunter also allowed himself to be interviewed for a January 1998 *New Yorker* article, which portrayed him as an embattled but reasonable man who was trying to grope his way toward a resolution of this maddening investigation.

Some people eased up on Hunter, but others did not. In December 1997, Fleet White, still enraged because the D.A. would not completely clear him of any suspicion, asked both Colorado Governor Roy Romer and Attorney General Gale Norton to remove Hunter from the case and appoint a special prosecutor. When they refused, White wrote a long letter to Boulder's *Daily Camera,* in which he vented his feelings and restated his wishes. These maneuvers were curious, but consistent with his earlier actions. The D.A., like John Ramsey before him—when White had insisted that Ramsey be more cooperative with the police—would not do what the oil man wanted. It seems that White had repeatedly gone out of his way to draw attention to himself, but why? Did he hold some clue to the Ramseys' guilt or innocence? Was he just an angry man, or was there some other reason?

Meanwhile, the Boulder police began canvassing the Ramseys' neighborhood and looking for a stun gun, a small weapon about the size of a TV remote control that emits a high-voltage shock. When this electric pulse hits the neuro-muscular system, it immobilizes an adult human being for several minutes and a child for even longer. After examining the autopsy photos, Lou Smit had noticed a pair of superficial abrasions on JonBenet's chin and two others on her back. The marks in both places were all but identical—round, rust-to-slightly-purple disfigurations. The space between them was also the same. To Smit, they looked like the tiny wounds left by the electrodes of a stun gun. He learned from stun gun manufacturers that the gaps between the marks were consistent with those created by the prongs of an Air Taser. The Ramseys claimed never to have owned a stun gun, although an instructional video for such a weapon was found among the nearly two hundred videotapes taken from their home. The cops were trying to link the gun to someone outside the family.

In February 1998, for the first time, Hunter publicly blasted the Ramseys for not working more closely with the police and his office. Months of frustration and anger, and the basic contradictions of the case, had finally erupted. Hunter was confronted with parents who were not assisting him in solving the murder of their daughter. He was also confronted with evidence—more of it than had been presented to the media—that pointed away from the Ramseys, even away from their friends, and in the direction of a larger, darker, uglier world that led outside of Boulder itself, one that was very difficult to penetrate and explore. Hunter was asking for help and finding that help extremely hard to come by.

On April 30, 1998, one year to the day after the Ramseys had finally agreed to a formal police interrogation, I sat down with Lou Smit at the Boulder County Justice Center. The ruddy-faced, soft-spoken, retired Colorado Springs detective repeatedly told me that he had seen all the evidence, that this was a "very complicated" murder, that no two people had ever been investigated more thoroughly than John and Patsy Ramsey, and that "it just isn't there." He implied that the person who took JonBenet's life remains unknown.

"The murderer is still walking around somewhere," he said. "A nasty individual took away this little girl's life and that's the kind of person we're looking for."

In June 1998, *Globe* freelancer Jeff Shapiro was having a beer in a Boulder tavern with Michael Tracey, the British journalism professor at the University of Colorado who produced the documentary about the case. Tracey held passionate convictions that the tabloids and mainstream media had wronged the Ramseys and he repeatedly voiced this to Shapiro. The intensity of the feelings he expressed had a great effect on the young reporter.

Although Shapiro had recently gotten a raise (from $750 to $1,000 a week), his luck had run somewhat colder since the death of the Princess of Wales.

"Dude," he told me on the phone not long after that fatal car wreck, "people don't want to talk to me anymore because I work for a tabloid. They're blaming us for what happened to that woman. This really sucks."

Shapiro was not used to being an object of scorn and derision or facing loose and unsubstantiated allegations against himself and those he worked for. He was discouraged.

"We're just doing our jobs," he said. "Don't people understand that?"

"Apparently not," I replied.

"What should I do?"

"Try to learn something from your experience."

Now, sitting in the bar with Tracey, he had a revelation.

"I suddenly realized," Shapiro told me later, "how much

pain we had caused the family. Michael made me see that. I told him that I knew John Ramsey was innocent of being a sexual abuser or a murderer. I looked everywhere for evidence that he was a pedophile, but it wasn't there. I found twenty people in Michigan who'd known John Ramsey for a long time and I interviewed all of them and found nothing bad.

"While Tracey and I were talking, I broke down into tears and just sat there and cried. Then I wrote John Ramsey a thirty-page letter telling him what I'd realized. Before sending the letter, I called him at home and said that I knew he was innocent and I apologized for any harm I'd caused his family. I called him a week later and left a message with Patsy. He called me right back and we talked for an hour. He was quiet on the phone. I talked mostly. He was definitely intrigued by anything I had to say about Fleet White and he laughed when I told him how I'd been tailing Fleet one time and Fleet had noticed me and started chasing me in his car. John told me that when all of this was over, he would hold some people in the media accountable. He never responded to my letter."

During this time, Shapiro also called Police Chief Tom Koby and told him that he now believed that his behavior had hurt people. When Shapiro said that he felt "sick inside," Koby replied that that was because "you have no principles," and that it was not the media's role to decide that someone was guilty of a crime and then try to prove that guilt. Koby told Shapiro something else, which echoed his comments at his January 9, 1997, press conference, in which he had said that the less you know about an event, the easier it is to give advice.

"This case," Koby told Shapiro, "isn't about good guys and bad guys and some day you will learn that."

33

For seventeen months, Alex Hunter had patiently waited. Then on June 1–2, 1998, the Boulder Police Department wrapped up its work and presented its evidence to the D.A. The next morning, exactly one year after Tim Honey had resigned as Boulder's city manager and Hunter had expressed concern to me about a sex scandal in his town, the D.A. finally took over the investigation. He put his own people on the street to dig into something that had intrigued him for a very long time: child pornography. Starting with the F.B.I., he used the appropriate people to do his legwork; the federal agents cast a wide net over a number of potential suspects in different locales. Despite a year and a half of resistance toward his leadership and unrestrained criticism of him, Hunter cooperated with the cops and the investigation lurched forward.

In late June, John and Patsy Ramsey voluntarily flew in from Atlanta for twenty hours of separate interviews with the authorities. Meanwhile, Detective Steve Thomas, one of the original police investigators on the case, requested a medical leave of absence from the department. Like his friend Fleet White, Thomas had been upset with Hunter almost from the start, but publicly had kept his feelings to himself. He would remain silent for another six weeks, until August 6, 1998, which would have been JonBenet's eighth birthday. On that date he released to his boss, Mark Beckner, a blistering resignation letter, in which he accused the D.A.'s office of hounding innocent people who should have been cleared long ago. He also noted an unresolved conflict of interest in the case that was marked by close relationships with the Ramsey attorneys, neglect of evidence, failure to pursue justice, and the myriad other things the cops had been carping about privately for more than a year. Like White, he also asked for a special prosecutor to step in and take over the investigation.

When Detective Thomas wrote this letter, which instantly became national news, Hunter was with his family on a ship off the coast of Alaska and could not be reached immediately. It would take several days for him to receive and absorb all that the former detective had written.

"It is my belief," Thomas wrote, "the district attorney's office has effectively crippled the case. The time for intervention is now. It is difficult to imagine a more compelling situation for the appointment of an entirely independent prosecution team to be introduced into this matter, who would oversee an attempt at righting this case. . . .

"On June 26, after leaving the investigation for the last time . . . I wept as I drove home, removing my detective's shield and placing it on the seat beside me, later putting it in a desk drawer at home, knowing I could never put it back on. . . . I realize that although I may have to trade my badge for a carpenter's hammer, I will do so with a clear conscience."

Faced with the greatest public assault on his credibility thus far, Hunter did not answer Thomas's charges, but held his silence and perservered. On August 12, six days after the letter was made public, the D.A. announced that, in order to further the investigation, the case was going to a grand jury so he could subpoena witnesses and compel them to testify under oath. A week later, after Colorado Governor Roy Romer and four district attorneys from the Denver area had reassured the media and the general population that the case was "on track" and that they were standing by Hunter and his prosecutorial team, Fleet White once again demanded Hunter's removal and tacitly accused John and Patsy Ramsey of not cooperating with the investigation. He then wrote yet another letter restating his position and continuing his offensive.

In late August, Patsy Ramsey's sister, Pamela, gave an interview to the *Rocky Mountain News* that was clearly designed to generate sympathy for the Ramseys. She contended that the murder had been a calculated effort by someone close to the family to destroy John and Patsy and mentioned all the hate mail the Ramseys had received since their daughter's death.

"I'm still taken aback," she said, "by all this bloodletting and need for flesh people have out there. I can't understand where that's coming from. And for some strange, horrible, awful reason, the flesh they want is ours."

A few days later, on September 1, Fleet White and his wife, Priscilla, stepped up their public offensive, showing up at a Boulder city council meeting. White exhorted council members, who did not know the evidence in the case, to pass a resolution endorsing or condemning the authorities' handling of the investigation. The city council declined.

As the date for convening the grand jury approached, the conflict and subtle public relations war between the Ramseys and Whites, which had begun at the time of the murder, was only growing more intense. Both the Ramseys and the Whites may have been completely innocent, but their behavior and the source of the tension between them—whatever it was—was raising intriguing questions.

The same day that the Whites appeared before the city council, a huge international Internet child porn ring, involving twelve countries and thirty-two American communities—including Fort Collins, Colorado, which is about an hour away from Boulder—was busted by the United States Customs Service. The agents raided the Fort Collins home of thirty-six-year-old Richard Bruce Thomes, who had recently left his job as chief financial officer of National Pet Care Centers, Inc., a chain of veterinary clinics, in order to start a computer consulting company. Thomes was suspected of involvement in child pornography and in the Wonderland porn club, which had as many as two hundred participants worldwide.

A few days after the bust, on September 5, the inherent difficulty and explosiveness of investigating this criminal realm was dramatically underlined. Thomes was found shot to death in his home; authorities believed it was a suicide. Then three other suspects, one in Connecticut, one in Maine, and another in Texas, also killed themselves.

34

One fall evening I drove out of Boulder on Highway 36 for the last time heading east to Denver. The questions surrounding the Ramsey case hung in the air like the ominous thunderheads that lay atop the Flatirons. Who had killed Jon-Benet . . . and why? What explained the stalemate that the investigation had become? What was below the surface of the case—the foreign DNA, parents who were reluctant to be interviewed by the police, a ransom note that made no sense? Could it be that the buildup to violence that resulted in Jon-Benet's murder lay within the business of exploiting the images of young children, and not the Ramsey family or its circle of friends? Was that why this homicide had such a hold on our consciousness?

When I reached the top of the hill overlooking the great valley that held the city, I pulled over to the shoulder. I turned off the engine and stepped outside, staring back at the town and the brownish vertical mountains that rise just behind it. The thunderheads shifted and split into black and blue and gray clouds, evoking the clash and strain of dramatic music working its way toward some resolution. The sky was charged and the mountains conjured up a volcano spewing smoke. Nestled up against this range were the community and the university; both kept pushing against the city limits and expanding into the foothills, like a finger of growth that could not be stopped.

Gazing down on Boulder, I remembered something I had read years before about certain cultures that had flourished centuries ago. At the time of the winter solstice, the ancients had believed that the late December sun, now resting at its low point in the heavens, would not come back to warm them and grow their food unless offerings were made to the gods. So they performed an annual ritual of sacrificing small children. Needing the light to survive, they struck a bargain with the unknown and kept it. The sun had always returned.

JonBenet had been killed at the end of December, in the dead of winter, at the coldest and darkest time of the year, when the sun was hanging low on the horizon. Her death had served as a reminder that children are not little adults but just children, who have almost no understanding of the grown-up world—even when we think they do. She has been gone over two years now and the light has not yet returned to Boulder.

Epilogue

Murder cases are like floating crap games. People who would never come together for any other reason suddenly converge and start to explore the mysteries of human violence—mysteries so deep that in some instances you can know all the relevant facts of a homicide and still not know the truth. Friendships are formed and enemies made. Lives are altered forever by the death of someone you had never heard of when that person was alive. Cases haunt your dreams and never fade away. The stabbing at truth goes on and on, if only in your head. The dead leave countless thoughts and feelings behind.

On September 15, 1998, the grand jury began meeting twice a week to hear the evidence. The word coming out of Boulder was that the authorities intended to present information to the jurors that would lead to the indictment of one or both of the Ramseys, not because they were certain they were guilty of murder, but in order to force them to talk. If the grand jury failed to indict anyone, then the case might be put to rest and the D.A. could say that he had tried but produced no results.

In late February 1999, nearly two years after we'd first spoken, I phoned Alex Hunter at his home. By this time, the grand jury had been meeting in Boulder for almost six months. Constant media reports predicted that it was about to end its work and come to some resolution.

"Is it too late," I asked the D.A., "for you to look into new information?"

"It's absolutely not too late to investigate new things," he said. "I'm not going to turn my head on anything. All doorways should come to our attention and need to be checked out. We've been criticized for operating this way, but that is how the prosecution works." I made an appointment to see him on Monday morning, March 1.

It was a very warm, late winter day in Boulder, and the trees looked strangely bare in such good weather. The new year had been extremely dry and the water flow in the creek next to the Justice Center was down to a trickle. It was odd walking back into Hunter's office so long after I'd first spoken with him there, in April 1997, and odder still to realize how little had changed in the Ramsey case during that time.

One of Hunter's investigators, Linda Wickman, joined us, and I told them that a month earlier I had appeared on a nationally and internationally broadcast live radio/live Internet show devoted to the Ramsey case. I had suggested on-air that JonBenet had been exposed to a subculture that reached far beyond her family and whose borderline pornographic and violently criminal activities exploited young children.

Two weeks later, a listener informed me of the arrest of an individual who knew people connected to JonBenet's murder and who was very upset about her death. This middle-class and technologically sophisticated man had been imprisoned for committing numerous crimes against children.

I visited him in jail one afternoon in mid-February. He looked very much the way I'd pictured him: overweight, sagging, and soft. He had a weak mouth and was pale and nondescript, except for his eyes. They were narrow, hurt, and fearful, difficult to gaze into or away from. They were dull and very, very sad.

He wanted to talk, and referred me to his lawyer. "I never did anything with children," he said, "except be too permissive. With just one child. That's all it was." Two hours later, I was sitting with his attorney in his office, discussing how his client's information might be useful in prosecuting the Ramsey case and in negotiating a deal to reduce his charges.

As I described these events, Hunter asked a number of questions about the inmate's legal status. He was cautious and skeptical, but said he would move forward with this lead.

"Is there anything else you can tell us?" he asked, looking as desperate for information as he had back in April 1997. The thing about Alex Hunter I will always remember is that he seemed genuinely hungry for more clues, for anything that would allow him to solve the case.

The following day, the inmate's lawyer called Boulder defense attorney Lee Hill, who had also worked as a prosecutor. His client was ready to talk and "wanted to help himself." The lawyer had already told his local D.A. that his client had been approached about the Ramsey matter and was now willing to speak to the authorities about the homicide. I phoned Hunter's office and left a message for him to call me at once. Hill then phoned the deputy D.A. prosecuting the inmate, who gave him two numbers to be passed along to Hunter.

At 3:30 P.M., Hunter returned my call and I gave him the numbers Hill had given me. "Thanks for being persistent," he said. "I'll call out there now."

As I hung up, it occurred to me that for two years the big question in Boulder had been whether the D.A.'s office wanted to break open the Ramsey case—or bury it. For two years, Hunter had been accused of not taking action. Silence had been his mode, at least in public. Now someone in jail wanted to speak to the right people about the killing, and now it was the D.A.'s turn to act, to free himself from the grasp of a murder case that had enveloped him in its darkness.